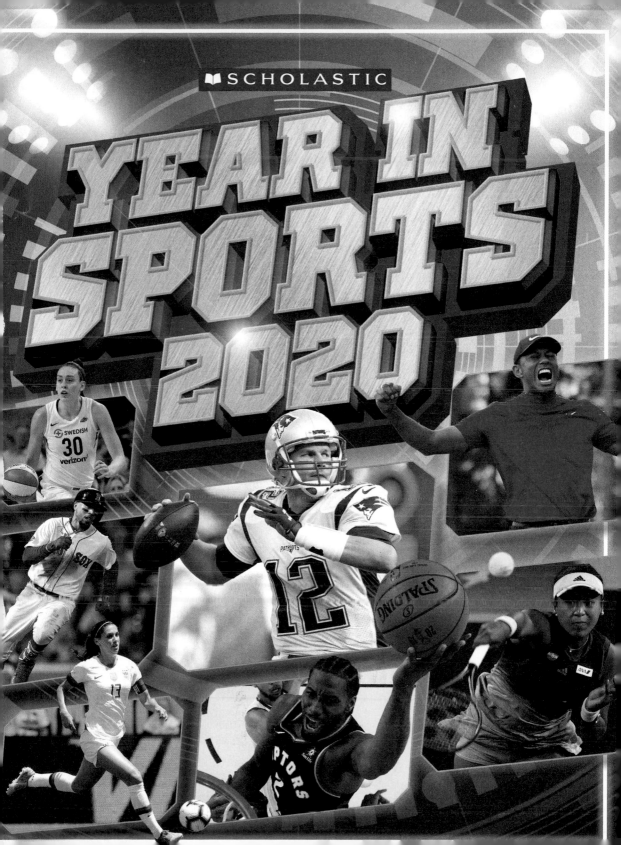

Copyright © 2019 by Shoreline Publishing Group LLC

All rights reserved. Published by Scholastic Inc., *Publishers since 1920*. SCHOLASTIC and associated logos are trademarks and/or registered trademarks of Scholastic Inc.

No part of this publication may be reproduced, stored in a retrieval system, or transmitted in any form or by any means, electronic, mechanical, photocopying, recording, or otherwise, without written permission of the publisher. For information regarding permission, write to Scholastic Inc., Attention: Permissions Department, 557 Broadway, New York, NY, 10012.

ISBN 978-1-338-56550-8

10 9 8 7 6 5 4 3 2 1   19 20 21 22 23

Printed in the U.S.A.
First edition, November 2019

Produced by Shoreline Publishing Group LLC

Due to the publication date, records, results, and statistics are current as of mid-July 2019.

UNAUTHORIZED: This book is not sponsored by or affiliated with the athletes, teams, or anyone involved with them.

Contents

Sports World!

There used to be a TV show called *The Wide World of Sports*. It covered just about everything people did to compete in games of all kinds. Over the past *Year in Sports*, fans got a better look than ever at just what a wide world of sports we all enjoy! American fans certainly could focus on homegrown events such as the Super Bowl and World Series, but the international sports world played a bigger part than ever as we moved from late 2018 through 2019.

Two huge international events dominated the summer of 2019. The Women's World Cup created excitement on every continent, with more teams than ever sending excellent squads to the tournament. The United States came in as defending champ, but they had to work harder than ever to win. Women's soccer worldwide got a huge boost from the many great games (but it was nice to see

USA! USA! USA! America's super soccer stars were the champs!

the Americans win again, right?).

In England, another of the world's favorite sports held its own World Cup. The sport of cricket is not a huge deal in America, but more than two BILLION people around the world are fans of this bat-and-ball sport. The best teams gathered in Great Britain for a month-long tournament. Who won? Check out page 175!

India and Australia battle in cricket.

Basketball was invented in America in 1891 and all of the NBA's champions have come from the US . . . until 2019! The Raptors became the first international winner and celebrated with a parade in their hometown of Toronto, Ontario, Canada. The NHL champion was from America—congrats to the St. Louis Blues!—but the league MVP and top scorer was from far-off Russia.

NASCAR was once again an all-American sport, but Formula 1 captured the attention of tens of millions of international fans . . . and they saw a record-setting season! The IndyCar champ raced in the US, but hailed from New Zealand.

Baseball continues to watch international stars shine on the field, but the 2019 season opened with games played in Japan! The NFL remained America's most popular sport—and the Patriots remained the Super Bowl–champion team—but the league also sent its teams to play three games in London, England!

If you love international sports, then the upcoming *Year in Sports* is sure to hold lots more excitement. After all, in July 2020, it's time once again for the Summer Olympics!

Until then, however, sit back and flip through this book of memories of the *Year in Sports*. We hope your favorite stars are in here; if not, we hope you meet some new ones!

TOP 10 MOMENTS IN SPORTS

We wish we had room for a Top 20! The past year was packed with big wins, huge upsets, new champions, and returning heroes. From a long list of choices, here are the best moments in sports since our last edition, covering September 2018 through August 2019.

10 **SOFTBALL SUPER CYCLE**
*Hitting for the cycle means getting a single, double, triple, and home run; it's a pretty rare feat. Hitting for the home run cycle is almost unheard of! In February, **Danielle Gibson** of Arkansas did it, though. In a 15–3 win, she cracked a solo homer along with a two-run shot and a three-run shot. Add in a grand slam and you've got a day for the ages! Oh, did we mention she did all that in just four innings?!*

9 **SMALL BUT MIGHTY** *Simone Biles* stands only four feet, eight inches, but she's a giant in the world of gymnastics. In late 2018, she won her fourth straight all-around world championship, becoming the first woman ever to do that! She earned other medals at the event to reach a record-tying career total of 20. Biles also became the first American woman with a world championship medal in every gymnastics event!

8 **THE STREAKY BEARD** *The streak started with a bang—50 points in a win over the Lakers in mid-December. And then Houston's **James Harden** just kept scoring . . . and scoring . . . and scoring! He poured in at least 30 points in each of his next 31 games to make it 32 in a row. That was the second-longest 30-point streak in NBA history, behind only the great Wilt Chamberlain's 65.*

7 POINTS GALORE! *The Kansas City Chiefs and Los Angeles Rams were supposed to play a November 2018 Monday Night Football game in Mexico City, which would have been historic. Instead, because of turf problems in Mexico, the game was played in LA and STILL made history! The offense-happy teams played "who can top this?" for four quarters. With a final score of 54–51 Rams, the teams scored the third-most combined points ever in an NFL game. It was the first game ever in which both teams went over 50!*

6

BOSTON'S BEST *The Boston Red Sox spent most of the 2018 season at the top of the AL standings. Their 108 wins set a team record, while their 592 extra-base hits led the league. AL MVP **Mookie Betts** became the first player to win a batting title while hitting 30 homers and stealing 30 bases. The team didn't lose four games in a row once all season; that matched a record set by the 1903 and 2013 Red Sox. But the most important number? No. 1. That's where the Sox finished after winning their fourth World Series since 2004.*

5 SINGING THE BLUES IN A GOOD WAY!

St. Louis has been playing in the National Hockey League since 1967. Before 2019, they had only reached the Stanley Cup Final once . . . and that was 49 years ago! So when they hoisted Lord Stanley's Cup after beating the Boston Bruins in seven games, you won't be surprised that their hometown threw them a pretty huge party! The story was even better, though, when you remember that in mid-January, St. Louis was in last place in the league. What a comeback!

4

CHAMPIONS OF THE NORTH *The NBA has been a two-country league since 1995. That's when the Toronto Raptors and the Vancouver (later Memphis) Grizzlies joined. However, until 2019, all the champions had come from the US. That changed when the mighty **Kawhi Leonard** headed north and carried the Raptors to their first NBA title. The Finals MVP was unstoppable, leading Toronto to a win over the three-time champion Golden State Warriors.*

3

A DOUBLE MIRACLE *Comebacks are pretty rare in soccer. They're even more rare in the two-game format most championships use. Teams play a game at each other's home stadium; the total goals scored determine the winner. So when Liverpool fell behind Barcelona in the Champions League semifinals, it looked like it was all over. Not so fast: Somehow, Liverpool (pictured) poured in four goals to overcome Barcelona. The second semifinal was even crazier! Tottenham Hotspur trailed Ajax Amsterdam 3–0 with just one half to go! Incredibly,* **Louis Moura** *of Tottenham scored three times to give his team the win on away goals.*

2

TIGER, TIGER, TIGER! *Sports fans love a comeback story. In 2019, they enjoyed a great one in golf.* ***Tiger Woods*** *was for many years the greatest player on the planet; some said he was the best ever. Back injuries and personal problems knocked him from the top, however. He had surgery and worked for years to regain his form, but fans wondered if he could make it back. At the 2019 Masters, he showed that he could. Woods won his fifth Masters and 15th Grand Slam event, second-most all-time. Yup, he's back!*

1

AMERICA'S BEAUTIFUL GAME *Our choice for the No. 1 event was easy! The US Women's Soccer Team beat the Netherlands 2–0 to win its fourth Women's World Cup. The victory capped a dominating performance in the month-long event. Millions of fans around the country followed every game, kick, goal, and quote, as the American team beat every opponent it faced. Being great is hard work; being great and winning even when everyone is out to stop you . . . that is really something special. The American women showed that they really are the gold standard for sports excellence.*

NFL

BIGGEST PLAY OF THE YEAR?
Super Bowl LIII seemed stuck in a defensive battle. The Los Angeles Rams and New England Patriots were tied 3–3 late in the fourth quarter. Then New England's Rob Gronkowski made this awesome, diving, 29-yard catch. It set up the game's only touchdown and helped the Pats bring home another championship.

A Season of Surprises

Every NFL season starts with all the teams at 0–0. In many years, fans and experts can predict much of what will happen. In 2018, however, a lot of predictions went out the window.

Minnesota and Jacksonville made the 2017 conference championships, so they figured to be in the thick of things again. Not so fast! Neither team made the playoffs! Philadelphia won the Super Bowl in the 2017 season, but struggled much of 2018, barely squeaking into the postseason. The Patriots lost two of their first three games; were they in trouble, too?

Chicago's defense was the key to 2018 success.

The Chicago Bears and Houston Texans were coming off last-place finishes. They hoped for some rebuilding. They got a lot more than that! Both teams went from worst to first in their divisions. The Texans became the first team ever to win nine straight games after losing their first three.

The Cleveland Browns had won only four games in the previous three seasons—combined! Would 2018 be more of the same? No, thanks to rookie QB **Baker Mayfield**. He led the team to its best season since 2007.

In Kansas City, **Patrick Mahomes** was handed the starting job. He was

Patrick Mahomes

1,371

NFL teams scored that many touchdowns in 2018, the most in any NFL season . . . ever! The teams also racked up 11,952 total points. That was the second-highest total in league history.

Other surprises included the Chargers, who played all their games in a tiny soccer stadium while their new home was being built. LA tied for the AFC's best record.

The other team in LA, the Rams, piled up the points and thrilled fans with exciting football. They earned a spot in Super Bowl LIII. In that game, however, the surprises stopped. The veteran Patriots showed that they still have what it takes to win. Led by G.O.A.T. **Tom Brady**, New England tied an NFL record with its sixth Super Bowl championship. What surprises will 2019 have in store for the NFL?

expected to have a slow start like most young QBs. Wrong again! Mahomes threw 30 TD passes in his first nine games—just shy of an NFL records—and ended up as the league MVP.

2018 Final Regular-Season Standings

AFC EAST	W	L	T	AFC NORTH	W	L	T	AFC SOUTH	W	L	T	AFC WEST	W	L	T
Patriots	11	5	0	Ravens	10	6	0	Texans	11	5	0	Chiefs	12	4	0
Dolphins	7	9	0	Steelers	9	6	1	Colts	10	6	0	Chargers	12	4	0
Bills	6	10	0	Browns	7	8	1	Titans	9	7	0	Broncos	6	10	0
Jets	4	12	0	Bengals	6	10	0	Jaguars	5	11	0	Raiders	4	12	0
NFC EAST	**W**	**L**	**T**	**NFC NORTH**	**W**	**L**	**T**	**NFC SOUTH**	**W**	**L**	**T**	**NFC WEST**	**W**	**L**	**T**
Cowboys	10	6	0	Bears	12	4	0	Saints	13	3	0	Rams	13	3	0
Eagles	9	7	0	Vikings	8	7	1	Falcons	7	9	0	Seahawks	10	6	0
Redskins	7	9	0	Packers	6	9	1	Panthers	7	9	0	49ers	4	12	0
Giants	5	11	0	Lions	6	10	0	Buccaneers	5	11	0	Cardinals	3	13	0

2018 Playoffs

Wild Card Weekend

If your favorite NFL team didn't make the playoffs in 2018, don't worry. It just might make it in 2019! In '18, seven of the eight teams that played on Wild Card Weekend had not been in the postseason a year earlier!

AFC: Colts 21, Texans 7

QB **Andrew Luck** led the Colts to three first-half scores before the Texans could get on the board. Indianapolis's defense did the rest, allowing only a single score. It was Indy's tenth win in 11 games.

AFC: Chargers 23, Ravens 17

San Diego mostly shut down hot QB **Lamar Jackson** by using seven defensive backs!

Chargers K **Michael Badgley** played a big part, nailing 5 field goals.

NFC: Cowboys 24, Seahawks 22

Seattle could not finish a late rally, and Dallas held on for a big win at home. QB **Dak Prescott** sneaked in for the final Cowboys' score, and then the hard-charging Dallas D kept **Russell Wilson** and the 'Hawks from coming back.

NFC: Eagles 16, Bears 15

The No. 6 seed Eagles upset NFC North-champion Chicago in the Bears' home. QB **Nick Foles** led Philly to a late score to take the lead. Chicago K **Cody Parkey** made what would have been a game-winning field goal, but the Eagles had called timeout. On the re-kick,

Dak dives! Prescott's late lunge toward the goal line set up a big TD in the Cowboys' win.

Parkey's attempt hit the upright AND the crossbar before bouncing out.

Divisional Playoffs

NFC: **Rams 30, Cowboys 22**

Pound it on the ground! That was the plan for the Rams, and it worked perfectly. RBs **C. J. Anderson** (123 yards and 2 TDs) and **Todd Gurley** (115 yards and 1 score) "rammed" through Dallas's D to lead LA to the NFC Championship Game. The Rams had 273 total rushing yards, the most ever given up by the Cowboys in 63 playoff games.

NFC: **Saints 20, Eagles 14**

Things looked bad for the Saints early in this game. The Eagles soared to a 14–0 lead. QB **Drew Brees** led the comeback, guiding his Saints on three long scoring drives. Philly looked like it might stage a comeback of its own, but an interception of a pass deflected by the Saints clinched the win.

AFC: **Chiefs 31, Colts 13**

Kansas City made it this far thanks to a high-powered offense. After this game, players gave their defense the credit. The Colts, led by QB **Andrew Luck**, had won 10 of 11 games coming into this one. The Chiefs held them to a single offensive touchdown: game over!

AFC: **Patriots 41, Chargers 28**

The Chargers played well; the Patriots played better. New England RB **Sony Michel** ran for three TDs. **Tom Brady** was his usual amazing self, leading the Pats to TDs on their first four possessions. The win sent New England to its record eighth straight AFC Championship Game.

Sony Michel scores for the Patriots.

Championship Games

NFC

Rams 26, Saints 23 (OT)

Saints fans will remember this for one play. Late in the game, the Saints were driving toward a go-ahead score. On a pass play near the goal line, interference should have been called on the Rams. (The NFL even admitted the mistake after the game.) That meant that after New Orleans made a field goal to take the lead, Rams QB **Jared Goff** had enough time left to lead his team to a game-tying field goal to force overtime. In the OT, the Rams hit **Drew Brees** as he threw a pass. They picked off the wobbly pass. A few plays later, Rams kicker **Greg Zuerlein** nailed a 57-yard field goal to win the game. The Rams headed to their first Super Bowl since the 2001 season.

You make the call: Was this interference?

AFC

Patriots 37, Chiefs 31 (OT)

For the first time ever, both conference championship games needed extra time. In the AFC game, though, only one team got the ball. The Patriots won the coin toss, and **Tom Brady** led one of his typical drives. **Rex Burkhead** bulled in from 2 yards out for the TD that won the game. Chiefs QB **Patrick Mahomes** continued his amazing season, however, by leading his team to the tying field goal late in the game. The exciting fourth quarter featured 38 points and four lead changes. The Pats headed to their NFL-record 11th Super Bowl.

The Patriots defense made a Ram sandwich of QB Jared Goff.

Super Bowl LIII

In the biggest game of the year, the Rams' defense just about shut down the Patriots' powerful offense. Los Angeles kept superstar QB **Tom Brady** in check, and the Pats scored only 13 points. So all that great work meant that the Rams won, right?

Wrong.

The Patriots' defense was even better! It hassled QB **Jared Goff** all night and stopped the Rams' high-scoring offense cold, allowing only a single field goal. The Rams punted each of the first eight times they had the ball!

The final result of this defensive battle was the lowest-scoring Super Bowl ever. New England beat the Rams 13–3.

Both teams combined to run only one play inside their opponents' red zone. That was the only touchdown of the game, scored by Pats RB **Sony Michel**. His 2-yard run in the fourth quarter came after a 29-yard strike from Brady to TE **Rob Gronkowski**. Gronk was triple teamed, but hauled in the catch near the goal line.

Other than that, there were few highlights in the game (although the Rams' **Johnny Hekker** did kick a Super Bowl-record 65-yard punt!). It was the first time in his nine Super Bowls that Brady did not have a TD pass. It didn't matter, as the Patriots came up with the perfect plan to stop the Rams.

The win gave the Patriots six Super Bowl titles, tied for the most ever with Pittsburgh. Brady became the first player to win six rings, too. For catching 10 passes for 141 yards, WR **Julian Edelman** was named the game's MVP.

2018 Stats Leaders

1,434 RUSHING YARDS
Ezekiel Elliott, Cowboys

17 RUSHING TDS
Todd Gurley, Rams

1,677 RECEIVING YARDS
Julio Jones, Falcons

125 RECEPTIONS
Michael Thomas, Saints

15 TD RECEPTIONS
Antonio Brown, Steelers

5,129 PASSING YARDS
Ben Roethlisberger, Steelers

50 TD PASSES
Patrick Mahomes, Chiefs

150 POINTS
37 FIELD GOALS
Ka'imi Fairbairn, Texans

◀◀◀**163** TACKLES
Darius Leonard, Colts

20.5 SACKS
Aaron Donald, Rams

7 INTERCEPTIONS
Kyle Fuller, Bears
Xavien Howard, Dolphins
Damontae Kazee, Falcons

NFL Awards

MOST VALUABLE PLAYER
PATRICK MAHOMES, QB
CHIEFS

DEFENSIVE PLAYER OF THE YEAR
AARON DONALD, DT
RAMS

OFFENSIVE ROOKIE OF THE YEAR
SAQUON BARKLEY, RB
GIANTS

DEFENSIVE ROOKIE OF THE YEAR
DARIUS LEONARD, LB
COLTS

COMEBACK PLAYER OF THE YEAR
ANDREW LUCK, QB
COLTS

COACH OF THE YEAR
MATT NAGY
BEARS

WALTER PAYTON NFL MAN OF THE YEAR
CHRIS LONG, DE
EAGLES

TOUCHDOWN CELEBRATION OF THE YEAR
SEATTLE SEAHAWKS

Saquon Barkley scored 11 TDs in his award-winning season.

1st Quarter

WEEKS 1-4

Fitzpatrick helped set an NFL record!

★ Hot Starts: Kansas City QB **Patrick Mahomes** threw 6 TD passes as the Chiefs held off the Steelers 42–37 in Week 2. That gave him 10 in the first two weeks, a new NFL record! New Orleans WR **Michael Thomas** set a new league record, too, catching 28 passes in his team's first two games.

★ Tough Day for Kickers: In Week 2, Cleveland K **Zane Gonzalez** missed four kicks in one game. The last would have given Cleveland a late lead. Instead, New Orleans kicker **Wil Lutz** smacked a game-winning 44-yarder with 21 seconds left. **Daniel Carlson** of Minnesota missed two kicks, both in overtime, and Minnesota and Green Bay tied 29–29. Gonzalez and Carlson were released the day after their games. Tough business!

★ Record Start: Tampa Bay beat New Orleans 48–40 in the opening game for both teams. It was the highest combined score for a season-opener in NFL history! The Bucs' **Ryan Fitzpatrick**, subbing for starter **Jameis Winston**, surprised everyone by throwing 4 TD passes and running for a score.

★ Undefeated!: That's what Cleveland fans could say for the first time after an opening weekend since 2004. The Browns didn't lose their opening game! Well, they didn't win, either. Cleveland and Pittsburgh tied 21–21.

★ Break Up the Bills!: After two losses, Buffalo rebounded with a big win over Minnesota, 27–6. The Vikings were favored by 17 points, making this the biggest upset in the NFL in 23 years. Buffalo rookie QB **Josh Allen** was the difference. He ran for two TDs and passed for a third. The Bills' defense forced three big turnovers, too.

★ New FG Champ: **Adam Vinatieri** of the Colts set a new NFL career record for field goals. He knocked through a 42-yard kick for this 566th three-pointer. That broke a tie with **Morten Andersen**. Unfortunately, Houston spoiled the day for Adam by winning 37–34 in overtime on— you guessed it—a field goal.

2nd Quarter
WEEKS 5-8

✱ Break Up the Browns, Too!: After an 0–16 2017 season, Cleveland started out 2018 in much better shape. In Week 5, the Browns ran their record to 2-2-1 with a 12–9 overtime win over the Ravens.

✱ New Yardage Champ: Drew Brees of the Saints threw a 62-yard TD pass to **Tre'Quan Smith** in New Orleans's 43–19 win over the Vikings. That pushed Brees ahead of **Peyton Manning** into first place on the NFL career passing yardage list. Brees's family was on hand to congratulate him.

✱ Battle of the Best: The AFC's top two teams met in a big Sunday-night showdown in Week 6. The back-and-forth battle featured 83 points, 8 TDs, and 9 field goals. The last of those three-point kicks was the difference. New England's **Stephen Gostkowski** nailed a 28-yard field goal as time ran out. That gave the Pats a 43–40 win over Kansas City.

✱ London Loves Football: And we don't mean soccer (though they love that, too, of course!). Fans there set an NFL attendance record for London, as 84,922 fans watched Seattle beat Oakland 27–3.

✱ A Scoring First: The Indianapolis Colts beat the Buffalo Bills 37–5. Why is that news? It was the first NFL game ever to end with that exact score!

✱ An Historic Miss: Baltimore's **Justin Tucker** had made 222 extra-point kicks without a miss . . . until Week 7. When the Ravens scored with 24 seconds left against the Saints, it looked like the game would head to overtime. Then Tucker shocked Ravens fans by slicing his kick outside the uprights. New Orleans won 24–23, and Tucker's streak was over!

✱ New Top Scorer: Vinatieri set another all-time mark. He became the NFL's all-time leading scorer, breaking the record of 2,544 career points. His 26-yard field goal in the Colts' 42–28 win over the Raiders put him over the top, knocking Andersen to second place again.

Brees shows his rank in all-time passing yards.

3rd Quarter
WEEKS 9–12

★ Vikings Sack Detroit: No, that's not a headline from the year 800. It is what Minnesota did to the Lions in Week 9. The Vikes set a team record with 10 sacks. The defense also scored on a fumble return to lead the team to a 24–9 win. It was the first time in 25 games that the Lions had not scored at least 14 points.

★ QB vs. QB: Tom Brady and **Aaron Rodgers** faced off for only the second time in their Hall of Fame careers. Of course, the two QBs aren't on the field at the same time, but the game was seen as a matchup of stars. Brady led his Patriots to a 31–17 win, though Rodgers and the Packers made a great comeback attempt late in the game.

★ Titans Triumph: Tennessee pulled off a big AFC upset by beating New England 34–10. The Titans' D shut down superstar **Tom Brady** with a big pass rush. Titans QB **Marcus Mariota** had 2 TD passes, while RB **Derrick Henry** banged into the end zone twice.

★ Big Ben!: Pittsburgh's **Ben Roethlisberger** has given his fans lots of great memories. His last-gasp dive into the end zone in Week 11 is one of the best. The Steelers' QB led a final-minute drive to Jacksonville's 1-yard line. With just seconds left, he rolled right and powered forward, stretching the ball out and into the end zone. His score gave the Steelers a 20–16 win.

On Target: In a 45–10 win over the Cardinals, San Diego QB **Philip Rivers** connected on 25 straight pass attempts and was 28 of 29 for the game. Both were new NFL records for the veteran passer. Three of his record-setting completions went for touchdowns.

Record-Setter!

The NFL's only 9–1 teams met in a huge Monday-night showdown. The game was played in LA after moving from Mexico City because of problems with the stadium turf there. It turned into one of the best regular-season games ever! Both teams poured points onto the board, but the Rams had more at the end, 54–51. It was the second-highest scoring game in NFL history, and the first time two teams each topped 50 points. The Chiefs also set the unhappy record of being the first team ever to score 50 or more points . . . and lose!

4th Quarter
WEEKS 13-17

✶ On a Roll: Houston started the season 0–3, and 2018 looked pretty bad for the team. But the Texans rallied . . . big time! With a 29–13 Week 13 win over Cleveland, they became the first team in NFL history to win nine straight after starting with three losses. Houston's D picked off three passes, and Texans QB **Deshaun Watson** had another good game.

✶ Play of the Year!: Down by five with seven seconds left and 69 yards from the end zone, Miami was in trouble against New England. Then **Ryan Tannehill's** pass to **Kenny Stills** turned–two laterals later– into the wildest play of the season and a stunning Dolphins win! Stills flicked the ball to **DeVante Parker**, who ran a few yards before tossing it to **Kenyan Drake**. Drake sped upfield and got a big block. Then he outran **Rob Gronkowski**–a tight end, of course, but brought in to knock down any long passes–to the end zone. That set off a loud celebration of a 34–33 win.

✶ Pick Free: Green Bay QB **Aaron Rodgers** set an NFL record with his 359th straight pass without an interception. As the cherry on top, the record-setting throw was a touchdown pass that helped the Packers beat the Falcons 34–20. Rodgers's streak ended later, after 403 pick-free passes.

✶ King Kittle: San Francisco TE **George Kittle** almost set a single-game record in a single *half*. Kittle pulled in seven passes for 210 yards in the first half against Denver, four yards shy of the single-game record for tight ends. Second half? Zero catches!

> **❝We work on [this play] in practice over and over. Sometimes it's like, 'Why are we doing this?' And now we know why!❞**
>
> —MIAMI WR
> **KENNY STILLS**

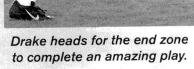

Drake heads for the end zone to complete an amazing play.

✶ Win . . . They're In!: In Week 17, the Colts beat the Titans 33–17 in a must-win game for both teams. The victory sent Indianapolis and QB **Andrew Luck** to the playoffs. Tennessee, meanwhile, went home for the offseason.

✶ Rookie Records: Young NFL stars made their mark with new records. **Baker Mayfield** threw 27 TD passes, most in a season by a rookie. **Saquon Barkley** made 91 receptions, most by a rookie running back. A pair of second-year stars also made the record books. **Christian McCaffrey's** 106 catches were the most ever for a running back. **Patrick Mahomes** became just the second player ever to pass for 5,000 yards and 50 TDs in a season.

2018: New Records

KEEPING IT CLOSE: Three points or fewer—that's how close 73 games ended in 2018. That was the most close games in a season ever! And if you liked comebacks, you got 71 of those (that is, coming back to win or tie in the fourth quarter or OT). That was the second-most of all time!

LIGHT UP THE SCOREBOARD: NFL teams combined to score 11,952 points. That was just 33 points behind the single-season record, set back in 2013. QBs threw the most PD passes ever, with 847, while setting a total completion percentage mark at 64.9.

KANSAS CITY KINGS: The Chiefs scored 565 of those points, the most by any team in the high-scoring 2018 season. It was also the third-most by a team ever in a single season.

RUNNING LIKE CRAZY: NFL players who carried the ball picked up an average of 4.42 yards per attempt. That, too, was an all-time NFL best. Not bad in a league that is more known these days for passing.

CATCHING ON: Speaking of passing, the NFL had 11 players each snag at least 100 catches. That was the most such players ever in a season. It broke the old record of 9 set in 1995. **Michael Thomas** of the Saints led the way with 125.

Michael Thomas

2019 NFL DRAFT TOP 10

RD.	PLAYER/SCHOOL/POS.	NFL TEAM
1	**Kyler Murray**, Oklahoma, QB	Cardinals
2	**Nick Bosa**, Ohio St., DE	49ers
3	**Quinnen Williams**, Alabama, DT	Jets
4	**Clelin Ferrell**, Clemson, DE	Raiders
5	**Devin White**, Louisiana St., LB	Buccaneers
6	**Daniel Jones**, Duke, QB	Giants
7	**Josh Allen**, Kentucky, LB	Jaguars
8	**T. J. Hockenson**, Iowa, TE	Lions
9	**Ed Oliver**, Houston, DE	Bills
10	**Devin Bush**, Michigan, LB	Steelers

2019 Hall of Fame

Welcome to these football people who joined the Pro Football Hall of Fame in 2019. Players marked with an * were elected in the first year in which they were eligible to join.

*Champ Bailey This outstanding cornerback made 12 Pro Bowls while playing with Washington (1999–2003) and Denver (2004–2013). He grabbed 52 interceptions and was considered the top "cover corner" during his time in the NFL.

Pat Bowlen bought the Denver Broncos in 1984 and turned them into Super Bowl champs. The team has won three NFL titles for him.

Gil Brandt was the secret weapon during the Dallas Cowboys' run of success from the late 1960s to the 1980s. He scouted new players and set up ways of working still used today. His teams won two Super Bowls and had 20 straight winning seasons.

*Tony Gonzalez was one of the top tight ends ever. His 1,325 catches are most ever for the position and second-most among all receivers.

Ty Law was another "stick-like-glue" cornerback of the early 2000s. He had his greatest years with the Patriots (1995–2004), with whom earned a pair of Super Bowl rings.

Kevin Mawae was the center on the NFL's All-Decade Team of the 2000s. His long career with the Seahawks, Jets, and Titans included blocking for 13 1,000-yard runners.

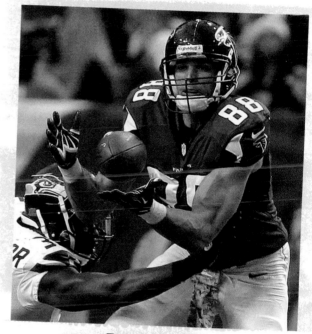

Tony Gonzalez

*Ed Reed was a hard-hitting ball hawk of a safety who was named the 2004 NFL Defensive Player of the Year. He set a record that year by returning his 9 interceptions for 358 yards.

Johnny Robinson started as a running back for the AFL's Dallas Texans but moved to safety. The team became the Chiefs, and Robinson helped them win two AFL titles and Super Bowl IV. He led his league in interceptions twice and had 57 for his career.

For the Record

Super Bowl Winners

GAME	SEASON	WINNING TEAM	LOSING TEAM	SCORE	SITE
LIII	2018	New England	L.A. Rams	13–3	Atlanta
LII	2017	Philadelphia	New England	41–33	Minneapolis
LI	2016	New England	Atlanta	34–28 (OT)	Houston
L	2015	Denver	Carolina	24–10	Santa Clara
XLIX	2014	New England	Seattle	28–24	Glendale, AZ
XLVIII	2013	Seattle	Denver	43–8	E. Rutherford, NJ
XLVII	2012	Baltimore	San Francisco	34–31	New Orleans
XLVI	2011	NY Giants	New England	21–17	Indianapolis
XLV	2010	Green Bay	Pittsburgh	31–25	Arlington, TX
XLIV	2009	New Orleans	Indianapolis	31–17	Miami
XLIII	2008	Pittsburgh	Arizona	27–23	Tampa
XLII	2007	NY Giants	New England	17–14	Glendale, AZ
XLI	2006	Indianapolis	Chicago	29–17	Miami
XL	2005	Pittsburgh	Seattle	21–10	Detroit
XXXIX	2004	New England	Philadelphia	24–21	Jacksonville
XXXVIII	2003	New England	Carolina	32–29	Houston
XXXVII	2002	Tampa Bay	Oakland	48–21	San Diego
XXXVI	2001	New England	St. Louis	20–17	New Orleans
XXXV	2000	Baltimore	NY Giants	34–7	Tampa
XXXIV	1999	St. Louis	Tennessee	23–16	Atlanta
XXXIII	1998	Denver	Atlanta	34–19	Miami
XXXII	1997	Denver	Green Bay	31–24	San Diego
XXXI	1996	Green Bay	New England	35–21	New Orleans
XXX	1995	Dallas	Pittsburgh	27–17	Tempe

GAME	SEASON	WINNING TEAM	LOSING TEAM	SCORE	SITE
XXIX	1994	**San Francisco**	San Diego	**49–26**	Miami
XXVIII	1993	**Dallas**	Buffalo	**30–13**	Atlanta
XXVII	1992	**Dallas**	Buffalo	**52–17**	Pasadena
XXVI	1991	**Washington**	Buffalo	**37–24**	Minneapolis
XXV	1990	**NY Giants**	Buffalo	**20–19**	Tampa
XXIV	1989	**San Francisco**	Denver	**55–10**	New Orleans
XXIII	1988	**San Francisco**	Cincinnati	**20–16**	Miami
XXII	1987	**Washington**	Denver	**42–10**	San Diego
XXI	1986	**NY Giants**	Denver	**39–20**	Pasadena
XX	1985	**Chicago**	New England	**46–10**	New Orleans
XIX	1984	**San Francisco**	Miami	**38–16**	Stanford
XVIII	1983	**LA Raiders**	Washington	**38–9**	Tampa
XVII	1982	**Washington**	Miami	**27–17**	Pasadena
XVI	1981	**San Francisco**	Cincinnati	**26–21**	Pontiac, MI
XV	1980	**Oakland**	Philadelphia	**27–10**	New Orleans
XIV	1979	**Pittsburgh**	Los Angeles	**31–19**	Pasadena
XIII	1978	**Pittsburgh**	Dallas	**35–31**	Miami
XII	1977	**Dallas**	Denver	**27–10**	New Orleans
XI	1976	**Oakland**	Minnesota	**32–14**	Pasadena
X	1975	**Pittsburgh**	Dallas	**21–17**	Miami
IX	1974	**Pittsburgh**	Minnesota	**16–6**	New Orleans
VIII	1973	**Miami**	Minnesota	**24–7**	Houston
VII	1972	**Miami**	Washington	**14–7**	Los Angeles
VI	1971	**Dallas**	Miami	**24–3**	New Orleans
V	1970	**Baltimore**	Dallas	**16–13**	Miami
IV	1969	**Kansas City**	Minnesota	**23–7**	New Orleans
III	1968	**NY Jets**	Baltimore	**16–7**	Miami
II	1967	**Green Bay**	Oakland	**33–14**	Miami
I	1966	**Green Bay**	Kansas City	**35–10**	Los Angeles

COLLEGE FOOTBALL

ORANGE POWER!
There is a lot of orange and black in this picture, but it's not Halloween! This was the confetti-covered scene after the Clemson Tigers knocked off Alabama to win the 2018 College Football Playoff. Read more about their win and the whole season inside!

Another Wild Season!

The past few seasons in college football have been like a tennis match. Alabama won in 2015, then Clemson was the 2016 champ. Then it was back to Alabama in 2017. So in 2018 it was . . . that's right! The Clemson Tigers.

On the way to that result, fans enjoyed a season packed with big games, upsets, and amazing performances. In this sport, the biggest question is usually, "Who's No. 1?" For most of the 2018 season, the question was, "Who will be No. 4?" The four-team College Football Playoff had three teams mostly locked up early on. Yes, the teams had to win some key late games, but the big three came through. Alabama, Clemson, and Notre Dame all rolled through the season undefeated to earn their spots in the playoff.

That left the fourth spot up for endless argument.

Ohio State made its case by winning the Big Ten. The Buckeyes boasted star QB **Dwayne Haskins**, who had a school-record 50 touchdown passes. However, a loss to Purdue hurt their chances.

Georgia hoped to return to the playoff, too. The Bulldogs lost to Alabama in the 2017 final. In 2018, they lost to Alabama in the SEC Championship Game. That knocked them out of the running for the national title.

The University of Central Florida went undefeated for the second regular season in a row, but could not crack the top four. Why not? The committee felt that it did not play in a conference as tough as the other teams. (UCF's winning streak came to an end in the Fiesta Bowl; see page 45.)

Fans of Texas, West Virginia, Kentucky, and Syracuse were happy to see their teams among the national rankings again, too.

In the end, the selection committee went with 12–1 Oklahoma as the fourth team, shutting out Ohio State and Georgia. The Sooners boasted an exciting, high-scoring offense led by Heisman Trophy

Dwayne Haskins

150

Happy birthday to pigskin! College football turns 150 years old in 2019, so look for celebrations of the game all season long. The first college game was played in 1869. Rutgers beat a school later known as Princeton 6–4. That game was more like rugby than today's football, but it kicked off one of America's favorite sports!

winner **Kyler Murray** (see box). The playoffs ended up on the same court as before, however, with Clemson facing Alabama across the net. Okay . . . enough tennis! Let's play football!

AWARDS

HEISMAN TROPHY (BEST OVERALL PLAYER)
DAVEY O'BRIEN TROPHY (TOP QB)
Kyler Murray/OKLAHOMA ▶

WALTER CAMP AWARD (TOP PLAYER)
MAXWELL AWARD (TOP ALL-AROUND PLAYER)
Tua Tagovailoa/ALABAMA

CHUCK BEDNARIK AWARD (TOP DEFENDER)
Josh Allen/KENTUCKY

OUTLAND TROPHY (BEST INTERIOR LINEMAN)
Quinnen Williams/ALABAMA

DICK BUTKUS AWARD (BEST LINEBACKER)
Devin White/LOUISIANA STATE

JIM THORPE AWARD (BEST DEFENSIVE BACK)
DeAndre Baker/GEORGIA

FRED BILETNIKOFF AWARD (BEST RECEIVER)
Jerry Jeudy/ALABAMA

DOAK WALKER AWARD
(BEST RUNNING BACK)
Jonathan Taylor/WISCONSIN

COACH OF THE YEAR
Brian Kelly/NOTRE DAME

August/September
SEASON HIGHLIGHTS

➔ **Whew!:** That's what No. 6 Penn State was saying after barely escaping a huge upset. The Nittany Lions needed overtime to defeat Appalachian State 45–38. That small school was already famous for a 2007 upset of mighty Michigan. No. 2 Clemson was also breathing a sigh of relief. In the Tigers' second game, they had to stop a two-point conversion try by Texas A&M with less than a minute to play. Clemson hung on to win 28–26.

➔ **Trojans Tumble:** No. 22 USC headed to Texas hoping to set itself up for a strong Pac-12 season. It turned out to be an ambush. The Longhorns whomped the

QB Ian Book led the Fighting Irish.

Trojans 37–14, thrilling their burnt-orange-covered fans.

➔ **Biggest Upset in Years!:** No. 127 beat No. 13! ESPN said that Old Dominion had a 1.8 percent chance to beat No. 13 Virginia Tech. Looks like ODU players don't watch ESPN! The Monarchs stunned the Hokies 49–35 thanks to QB **Blake LaRussa**. The team's backup, he came in during the first quarter and took off! He threw for 495 yards and 4 TDs.

➔ **The Old Army Try:** No. 5 Oklahoma escaped an upset of its own. The Sooners needed overtime to beat hard-charging Army 28–21. A goal-line stop by Army and a missed field goal by OU late in the fourth quarter set up the OT. Oklahoma sealed the deal with an interception on Army's overtime possession.

➔ **Here Come the Irish!:** No. 8 Notre Dame moved to 5–0 with a big win over No. 7 Stanford. The Fighting Irish dominated most of the game and shut down **Bryce Love**, Stanford's big-play back. ND won 38–17.

➔ **Buckeye Power:** The biggest crowd in Penn State history (110,889) went home disappointed as No. 4 Ohio State rallied to top the No. 9 Nittany Lions. The teams combined for 26 points in the fourth quarter, but OSU scored last. **K. J. Hill** caught a short pass and carried it 24 yards for the game-clinching TD with just over two minutes left. The 27–26 win kept the Buckeyes in the playoff hunt.

October
SEASON HIGHLIGHTS

→ **Sooner Showdown:** The game between Texas and Oklahoma is known as the Red River Rivalry, for the waterway that divides the two states. No. 19 Texas put a dent in No. 7 Oklahoma's playoff hopes with a 48–45 win. Texas QB **Sam Ehlinger** ran for three TDs and passed for two more. He also set up the game-winning field goal by **Cameron Dicker** with a late long pass.

→ **Little School, Big Upset:** Tiny Elon University was a 39-point underdog to James Madison, the No. 2 team in the lower-level FCS and a team that had won 20 straight games in the Colonial Athletic Association. Elon ignored the prediction and pulled off a huge upset, winning 27–24.

→ **Upset Saturday!:** It seems like it happens every year. A fall Saturday rolls around and the Top 10 gets scrambled. It happened this year on October 13. No. 2 Georgia was the biggest tree to fall, losing to No. 13 LSU 36–16. LSU moved up to No. 5 after the win. No. 6 West Virginia was upset by Iowa State 30–14, while Oregon needed overtime to beat No. 7 Washington 30–27. Perhaps the biggest surprise was No. 8 Penn State's 21–17 loss to Michigan State. The Spartans used a couple of trick plays to shock the Nittany Lions.

→ **Come-from-Ahead Loss:** Nebraska's nightmare season continued in October. The Cornhuskers moved to a shocking 0–6 after losing to Northwestern. The loss was even

The Golden Bears celebrated a big upset win!

tougher since they led by 10 with about three minutes left. Then they allowed the Wildcats to tie the game and win 34–31 in overtime.

→ **No. 2 Goes Down!:** Ohio State was shocked by unranked Purdue in one of the biggest upsets of the year. The Buckeyes had won 12 straight before getting swamped by the Boilermakers 49–20. Purdue scored four touchdowns in the fourth quarter to seal the win.

→ **Go Bears!:** No. 15 Washington's hopes for a spot in the Pac-12 Championship Game took a big hit when it was upset by California 12–10. Cal LB **Evan Weaver** returned an interception for the go-ahead score on a day when the Cal defense was the big story.

November
SEASON HIGHLIGHTS

Utah flew through the snow to defeat Colorado.

the University of San Diego. Bad news for Davidson: It lost the game 56–52. Even having four players with 150 or more rushing yards each was not enough for the W.

→ **Cowboys Say "Yee-Haw!":** A week after almost beating Oklahoma, Oklahoma State pulled off November 17's biggest upset, defeating No. 7 West Virginia 45–41. OSU QB **Taylor Cornelius** was excellent, throwing 5 TD passes. He also ran for a score. His game-winning TD strike came with less than a minute to go.

→ **Go for Broke!:** West Virginia put its No. 12 ranking on the line late in a game against Texas. With just 16 seconds left, the Mountaineers scored on a 33-yard TD pass. The extra point kick would have tied the game, but WVU went for two instead. QB **Will Grier** ran the ball in to give his team a brave 42–41 victory.

→ **Top Three:** Harvard has been playing football for 144 years. In all that time, they had never had a touchdown pass play longer than 74 yards. In a 52–18 win over Columbia, Harvard made THREE such plays–in the first quarter! QB **Tom Stewart** connected for passes of 74, 75, and 92 yards. They are the three longest plays in the school's long history!

→ **Rushing Record:** Good news for Davidson: The team set an NCAA record with 789 rushing yards in its game against

→ **Snow T.O.:** Usually, referees have to warn players about the rules. In the Utah-Colorado game, the ref had to warn the fans. He stopped the game in the second quarter to plead with fans to stop throwing snowballs onto the field! Perhaps the Colorado fans were upset because their team lost to Utah 30–7.

→ **Points and More Points:** A pair of games around Thanksgiving gave scoreboard operators a workout. No. 6 Oklahoma outlasted West Virginia 59–56. It seemed like both teams scored every time they had the ball! The next day, Texas A&M needed extra time to upset No. 7 LSU–a LOT of extra time. The two teams played seven overtimes, tying an NCAA record. The game finally ended when A&M made a two-point conversion for the final score of 74–72!

December
SEASON HIGHLIGHTS

CONFERENCE CHAMPIONSHIPS

SEC: Georgia almost pulled off a big upset over No. 1 Alabama, but backup QB **Jalen Hurts** was the hero for the Crimson Tide. He came in after starter **Tua Tagovailoa** was injured. Hurts threw for a TD and ran for the winning score. Alabama won the game 35–28 and earned a chance to repeat as national champs.

Big 12: Oklahoma got revenge for its only loss of the season. The Sooners beat Texas 39–27; they had lost to the Longhorns back in October. QB **Kyler Murray** threw for 379 yards and 3 TDs, but it was the OU defense that led the way. A key safety turned the game in Oklahoma's favor.

Big Ten: Ohio State made its case to join the playoff with a solid 45–24 win over No. 21 Northwestern. It was the Buckeyes' third title in five seasons. For the fifth time this year, QB **Dwayne Haskins** topped 400 yards passing. He had 499 yards in this game and threw for 5 TDs.

ACC: No. 2 Clemson continued on its season-long roll with a lopsided, 42–10 win over Pittsburgh. Even in the rain, the Tigers roared, rushing for a total of 301 yards and 4 scores.

Clemson's D held Pitt's passing attack to only 8 yards!

Pac-12: Defense ruled this game. The 13 combined points were the lowest ever in a conference championship game. Washington got 10 of them—seven on a pick-six—and held Utah to a field goal to win the title.

Kyler Murray romped over the Longhorns.

Bowl Bonanza!

PERFECT PASSING: In the Idaho Potato Bowl, the BYU Cougars mashed the Western Michigan Broncos 49–18. Mashed . . . get it? BYU QBs had a record-setting day. Starter **Zach Wilson** completed all 18 of his attempts. Backup **Tanner Mangum** was 1-for-1 in his short time on the field. That made BYU a perfect 19-for-19, a new record for a bowl game.

THE NO BOWL: Boston College led Boise State 7–0 in the opening quarter of the First Responder Bowl in Dallas when a thunder-and-lightning storm rolled into the area. Fans had to leave their seats for safety, while the players headed to the locker room. The weather stuck around so the game had to be canceled. It was thought to be the first bowl game cut short since 1941.

THE ICK BOWL: Cal and TCU played a bowl game that both teams probably *wish* had been canceled. The Cheez-It Bowl was one ugly football game. The teams combined for 9 interceptions. Six came in the first half, setting an all-time all-bowl record. The two teams managed only 2 TDs between them in four quarters. TCU had 28 yards passing . . . *in the game.* TCU could have won on the final play of the fourth quarter,

Goodbye, perfection! LSU squashed Central Florida's dream of another undefeated season.

The Other Playoffs

Most of the attention went to the big game between Clemson and Alabama. Other college football divisions end in playoffs, too, so let's celebrate these "little guys" who were best in their worlds.

Hardin-Baylor got revenge for a 2017 loss.

FCS: North Dakota State won a record seventh title (in eight seasons!) in this division, one level below the top. QB Easton Stick (what a cool name!) threw 2 TD passes and ran for 3 more scores. His team beat Eastern Washington 38–24.

Division II: Valdosta State held off Ferris State 49–47 in the highest scoring D-II championship game ever. Valdosta QB Rogan Wells set a title-game record by being responsible for 6 TDs (5 passing and 1 receiving). Each team also scored a TD on a trick play in a wild and entertaining game.

Division III: Try, try again—that was the theme of the D-III title game. The University of Mary Hardin-Baylor lost the 2017 final, but roared back to win in 2018. A 24–16 win over Mount Union gave UMHB a perfect 15–0 record. It also snapped D-III powerhouse Mount Union's 29-game winning streak!

NAIA: This small-school division still plays fierce football. Morningside (Iowa) won its first national title, knocking off Benedectine 35–28.

but missed a field goal attempt. Then in overtime, TCU was penalized when a team official fell onto the field and tripped a referee by accident. The Horned Frogs won 10–7, but this game will be remembered for how bad it was, not who won!

ROSE BOWL: Ohio State coach **Urban Meyer** ended a great career with a big win over Washington, 28–23. Buckeyes QB **Dwayne Haskins** passed for 3 TDs to finish an amazing season. The Huskies made it interesting, scoring 20 points in the fourth quarter, but they couldn't finish the comeback.

FIESTA BOWL: The streak is over! The University of Central Florida's 25–game winning streak ended as the LSU Tigers won 40–32. LSU QB **Joe Burrow** had 4 TD passes. As UCF tried to come back in the second half, LSU's D allowed only a field goal and a late TD.

SUGAR BOWL: Texas finished off a great rebound year with a 28–21 upset win over No. 5 Georgia. The Longhorns have had some tough seasons, but their fans stayed loyal. Texas QB **Sam Ehlinger** ran for 3 TDs. The game capped off the first 10-win season by Texas since 2009.

Tagovailoa did it all for Alabama and carried them to another shot at the national title.

2018 Semifinals

COTTON BOWL
Clemson 30, Notre Dame 3

Big plays: Clemson made them; Notre Dame didn't. Four long-distance scoring plays were the difference in this surprising blowout by the Tigers. Freshman QB **Trevor Lawrence** threw TD passes to **Justyn Ross** (52 and 42 yards) and **Tee Higgins** (19 yards). Higgins's catch was a one-handed highlight-reel showstopper that ended the first half. RB **Travis Etienne** put the capper on the game with a 62-yard run in the second half. Clemson earned its third trip to the title game in four seasons.

ORANGE BOWL
Alabama 45, Oklahoma 34

Alabama QB **Tua Tagovailoa** was nearly perfect, completing 24 of 27 passes for 318 yards and 4 touchdowns. He had a lot of help—nine different players caught at least one pass for Alabama. The defending champs led 28–0 in the first half, so the Sooners played catch-up all day. Oklahoma QB **Kyler Murray** did pretty well, leading the Tide to 34 points (the most given up by 'Bama all season), but it wasn't enough. Alabama's win set up its fourth showdown with Clemson in the past four seasons!

Tigers Roar!

2017 CHAMPIONSHIP

For the first few minutes of the College Football Championship Game, it looked like fans were in for a roller-coaster ride. After only nine minutes, it was 14–13 with Clemson on top of Alabama. Both teams had scored on long plays. Clemson got the scoring started with a 44-yard interception return. Then Alabama took a 16–14 lead early in the second quarter on a field goal. The game was speeding along . . . until Clemson changed gears.

After Alabama scored its 16th point, the Tigers roared—um, *scored* 30 points in a row while keeping the Crimson Tide

off the board. That amazing run led to a 44–16 rout. Clemson won its second national title in three years.

Freshman QB **Trevor Lawrence** led the way for Clemson. Only 19 years old, he played like an NFL veteran. Lawrence completed 3 TD passes while throwing for 347 yards. Lawrence kept his cool even as Alabama's defense tried to knock him back.

Lawrence got help from some amazing catches by his receivers. **Justyn Ross** made a pair of one-handed grabs on the sideline to keep a touchdown drive alive. **Tee Higgins** made a fingertip catch for the final touchdown.

Clemson also got a huge game from RB **Travis Etienne**. He scored twice on the ground and once on a pass from Lawrence.

Meanwhile, Clemson's D shut down Heisman Trophy runner-up **Tua Tagovailoa**. The Alabama QB had only four interceptions all season; Clemson picked him off twice! He was pressured and pushed all night long.

With Clemson and Alabama splitting the past four titles . . . will they go for a five-peat of their battle in January 2020?

Lawrence was lights-out for Clemson.

We're No. 1!

These are the teams that have finished at the top of the Associated Press's final rankings since the poll was first introduced in 1936.

SEASON	TEAM	RECORD	SEASON	TEAM	RECORD
2018	Clemson	15–0	1976	Pittsburgh	12–0
2017	Alabama	13–1	1975	Oklahoma	11–1
2016	Clemson	14–1	1974	Oklahoma	11–0
2015	Alabama	14–1	1973	Notre Dame	11–0
2014	Ohio State	14–1	1972	USC	12–0
2013	Florida State	14–0	1971	Nebraska	13–0
2012	Alabama	13–1	1970	Nebraska	11–0–1
2011	Alabama	12–1	1969	Texas	11–0
2010	Auburn	14–0	1968	Ohio State	10–0
2009	Alabama	14–0	1967	USC	10–1
2008	Florida	13–1	1966	Notre Dame	9–0–1
2007	LSU	12–2	1965	Alabama	9–1–1
2006	Florida	13–1	1964	Alabama	10–1
2005	Texas	13–0	1963	Texas	11–0
2004	USC	13–0	1962	USC	11–0
2003	USC	12–1	1961	Alabama	11–0
2002	Ohio State	14–0	1960	Minnesota	8–2
2001	Miami (FL)	12–0	1959	Syracuse	11–0
2000	Oklahoma	13–0	1958	LSU	11–0
1999	Florida State	12–0	1957	Auburn	10–0
1998	Tennessee	13–0	1956	Oklahoma	10–0
1997	Michigan	12–0	1955	Oklahoma	11–0
1996	Florida	12–1	1954	Ohio State	10–0
1995	Nebraska	12–0	1953	Maryland	10–1
1994	Nebraska	13–0	1952	Michigan State	9–0
1993	Florida State	12–1	1951	Tennessee	10–1
1992	Alabama	13–0	1950	Oklahoma	10–1
1991	Miami (FL)	12–0	1949	Notre Dame	10–0
1990	Colorado	11–1–1	1948	Michigan	9–0
1989	Miami (FL)	11–1	1947	Notre Dame	9–0
1988	Notre Dame	12–0	1946	Notre Dame	8–0–1
1987	Miami (FL)	12–0	1945	Army	9–0
1986	Penn State	12–0	1944	Army	9–0
1985	Oklahoma	11–1	1943	Notre Dame	9–1
1984	Brigham Young	13–0	1942	Ohio State	9–1
1983	Miami (FL)	11–1	1941	Minnesota	8–0
1982	Penn State	11–1	1940	Minnesota	8–0
1981	Clemson	12–0	1939	Texas A&M	11–0
1980	Georgia	12–0	1938	Texas Christian	11–0
1979	Alabama	12–0	1937	Pittsburgh	9–0–1
1978	Alabama	11–1	1936	Minnesota	7–1
1977	Notre Dame	11–1			

NATIONAL CHAMPIONSHIP GAMES

Until the 2014 season, there was no national championship playoff system at the highest level of college football. From 1998 to 2013, the NCAA ran the Bowl Championship Series, which used computers and polls to come up with a final game that pitted the No. 1 team against the No. 2 team. The new system, called the College Football Playoff, has a panel of experts that sets up a pair of semifinal games to determine which teams play for the national title. Here are the results of BCS and College Football Playoff finals since 2000.

SEASON	TEAMS AND SCORE	SITE
2018	**Clemson 44, Alabama 16**	SANTA CLARA, CA
2017	**Alabama 26, Georgia 20** (OT)	NEW ORLEANS, LA
2016	**Clemson 35, Alabama 31**	TAMPA, FL
2015	**Alabama 45, Clemson 40**	GLENDALE, AZ
2014	**Ohio State 42, Oregon 20**	ARLINGTON, TX
2013	**Florida State 34, Auburn 31**	PASADENA, CA
2012	**Alabama 42, Notre Dame 14**	MIAMI, FL
2011	**Alabama 21, LSU 0**	NEW ORLEANS, LA
2010	**Auburn 22, Oregon 19**	GLENDALE, AZ
2009	**Alabama 37, Texas 21**	PASADENA, CA
2008	**Florida 24, Oklahoma 14**	MIAMI, FL
2007	**LSU 38, Ohio State 24**	NEW ORLEANS, LA
2006	**Florida 41, Ohio State 14**	GLENDALE, AZ
2005	**Texas 41, USC 38**	PASADENA, CA
2004	**USC 55, Oklahoma 19**	MIAMI, FL
2003	**LSU 21, Oklahoma 14**	NEW ORLEANS, LA
2002	**Ohio State 31, Miami (FL) 24** (2 OT)	TEMPE, AZ
2001	**Miami (FL) 37, Nebraska 14**	PASADENA, CA
2000	**Oklahoma 13, Florida State 2**	MIAMI, FL

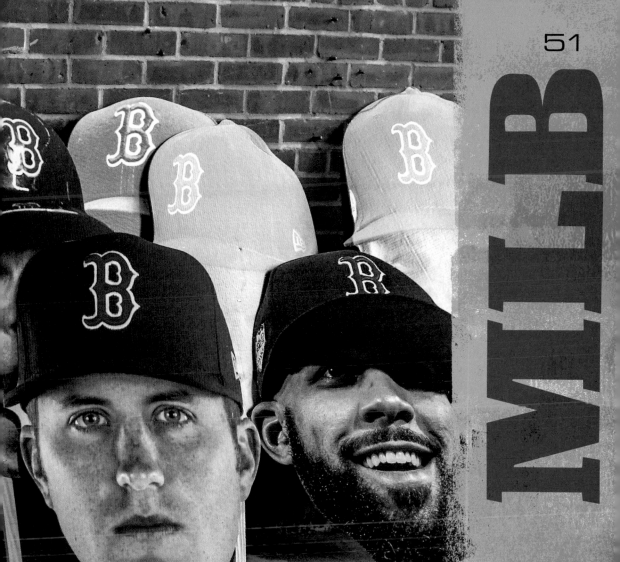

MLB

HEAD'S UP, SOX!
Big-head posters of Boston Red Sox players wait to be carried in a victory parade. Why? Because the Sox captured their fourth World Series championship since 2004 by beating the Los Angeles Dodgers. Read all about it inside!

Big, Bad Boston

You might think that the MLB team with the best record ends up winning the World Series, right? Well, there have been 49 World Series since baseball started having playoffs. (Before that, the top AL team played the top NL team; no playoffs!) The team with the best overall regular-season record has won only 13 of those 49 times! It's not how you start . . . it's how you finish!

One franchise has done that three times. The Boston Red Sox set a team record with 108 regular season victories and went to win their fourth World Series of the 2000s. They also pulled off the best-record/World Series double in 2007 (tie) and 2013. If you add in their playoff wins, they won 119 games in 2018. That's the second-most all-time behind the 1998 New York Yankees. It was a great year to be a Sox fan!

The 2018 season had lots of other great stories, however. Both leagues included teams that surprised many

experts by putting up great numbers. The top record in the NL belonged to the Milwaukee Brewers. The "Brew Crew" used a great bullpen with some solid hitters to make their first playoffs since 2011. In Atlanta, the Braves had one of baseball's youngest lineups. A half dozen of its regular players were younger than 25. Yet the "kids" easily won the NL East. Watch for this young Atlanta team to keep making noise!

In the AL, the Tampa Bay Rays won 90 games. They did so using a new type of pitching strategy. In many games, they used a relief pitcher to "open" the game. He might only pitch an inning against an opponent's top hitters. Then he'd leave for a long reliever. Of course, the Rays also had a "traditional" starter named **Blake Snell** who led the AL with 21 wins! On a list of how much teams pay their players, the Oakland Athletics are near the bottom. In

NL MVP
Christian Yelich

Khris Davis was an Oakland slugger.

.248

That's the batting average for all Major League players in 2018. Not that great, right? It was the lowest mark since the 1972 season. A big reason? More players are striking out than ever before (see page 55).

2018, they played like a very expensive ball club! Big hitters like **Khris Davis** and **Matt Olson** paced a scrappy team that earned a wild-card playoff spot.

At the top of the big-spenders list, though, the Red Sox, Los Angeles Dodgers, and Chicago Cubs all made it to the playoffs as expected. It took the Dodgers an extra game, though. The players in Major League Baseball had so much fun in 2018 they

didn't want it to end! For the first time, there were *two* tiebreakers in the National League. So four teams got to play a bonus, 163rd game! The Dodgers and Brewers each had to win one of those to earn division titles.

As you'll see on page 55, MLB players also continued a surprising trend. Quiz time: Do you think there were more hits or strikeouts in 2018? Read on to find out!

2018 REGULAR SEASON STANDINGS

AL EAST		AL CENTRAL		AL WEST	
Red Sox	108–54	Indians	91–71	Astros	103–59
Yankees	100–62	Twins	78–84	Athletics	97–65
Rays	90–72	Tigers	64–98	Mariners	89–73
Blue Jays	73–89	White Sox	62–100	Angels	80–82
Orioles	47–115	Royals	58–104	Rangers	67–95

NL EAST		NL CENTRAL		NL WEST	
Braves	90–72	Brewers	96–67	Dodgers	92–71
Nationals	82–80	Cubs	95–68	Rockies	91–72
Phillies	80–82	Cardinals	88–74	Diamondbacks	82–80
Mets	77–85	Pirates	82–79	Giants	73–89
Marlins	63–98	Reds	67–95	Padres	66–96

Around the Bases 2018

Streaky Pitcher: Mets ace **Jacob deGrom** got on a hot streak on April 16 . . . and never stopped. By the end of the season, he had put together a streak of 29 starts allowing only three earned runs or fewer. That was the longest single-season streak in big-league history!

Young Stars: Atlanta featured a lot of great young players, but two stood out. **Ronald Acuña** became the youngest player ever with homers in five straight games. He ended up with 26 on the season. Teammate **Ozzie Albies** had 24. Together, they were the first teammates under 22 years old to each have 20 or more homers in the same season.

Weird Walk-Offs: Houston 3B **Alex Bregman** had two game-winning walk-off "hits." Together they traveled about 30 feet! In April, he hit a huge pop fly that would have ended the 10th inning of a tie game. But the Padres let it fall in front of the mound and Houston scored the winning run! In July, Bregman's 11th-inning dribbler just in front of the plate caused problems. First, the catcher for Oakland tried to pick it up and tag Bregman. He missed! On the throw to first, the ball hit Bregman and bounced away. His Houston teammate raced in with the winning run! Wild!

One Batter, Two Fielders, Three Outs: In an August game against the Angels, the Rangers did something baseball hasn't seen in 106 seasons! With the bases loaded, Texas third baseman **Jurickson Profar** snagged a one-hop grounder from LA's **David Fletcher**. Profar stepped on third for one out. Then he tagged the runner on third, who had stayed near the bag thinking Profar had caught the ball in the air. Profar then threw to second baseman **Rougned Odor** to force the runner coming from first. It was the first triple play that did not include the batter being out since 1912!

Jacob deGrom

COOL 2018 STATS

* For the first time in history, MLB players had more strikeouts than hits. They combined for 41,207 Ks and 41,020 hits. What's going on? Many players are changing their swings to try to hit homers. Unfortunately, they often miss!

* MLB teams set a new record for position players taking the mound. In all, non-pitchers were called in for mop-up duty 48 times in 2018. That's way more than the previous record.

* The Yankees' 267 home runs were the most by a team in a single season in MLB history. They were also the first to have at least 20 homers from every spot in the batting order!

* Boston's **Mookie Betts** became the first player to have 30 steals and 30 homers while also winning the league batting title!

* **Christian Yelich** of the Brewers missed winning the NL Triple Crown by only one RBI and two home runs! He did win the NL batting title, though.

Betts was double trouble for Boston's foes.

Fooled Ya!: It takes a lot to fool a big-league umpire, but the Mets' **Todd Frazier** managed to do it in a September game. The veteran third baseman had to fall into the first row while chasing a foul pop. He came holding up a ball that he showed to the ump, who called the batter out. Frazier then tossed the ball back into the stands. Turns out he had grabbed a rubber practice ball instead of the real one! He confessed after the game, but it made a lot of highlight shows.

So Long, Scioscia: The Angels said goodbye to longtime manager **Mike Scioscia**. He resigned from the team after 19 seasons. Scioscia was the longest-serving manager in the big leagues and was tied for sixth all-time in seasons with one club. He led the team to their only World Series win in 2002 along with six other playoff seasons.

2018 MLB Playoffs

ALDS

Red Sox 3, Yankees 1

Boston won two straight at Yankee Stadium to clinch a spot in the ALCS. The first of those was a 16–1 pasting. In that game, Boston's **Brock Holt** became the first player ever to hit for the cycle in a postseason game. The series clincher came down to a bang-bang play at first base for the final out as Boston returned to the ALCS for the first time since 2013.

Astros 3, Indians 0

Houston rolled over Cleveland, outscoring them a combined 21–6. Houston

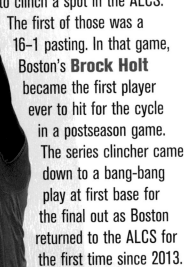

Springer hit three dingers!

OF **George Springer** hit three home runs, including two in the series-clinching Game 3, while Houston's powerful pitching shut down the Cleveland offense.

NLDS

Milwaukee 3, Colorado 0

The Brewers came into the series knowing they had to outpitch the hard-hitting Rockies. The Brew Crew came through. Milwaukee pitchers allowed only two runs in three games and the Brewers swept the series.

Dodgers 3, Braves 1

The Dodgers used great starting pitching to pace a series win. **Hyun-Jin Ryu** went seven innings in a 6–0 opening-game win.

Clayton Kershaw went one better in Game 2, pitching eight shutout innings as the Dodgers won 3–0. After an Atlanta win, LA clinched the series with a 6–2 win, helped by a **Manny Machado** three-run homer.

ALCS
Red Sox 4, Astros 1

Even though Boston had won a team-record 108 games, many experts favored the Astros in this series. Houston was the defending champ, after all, and had great starting pitchers. Game 1 went Houston's way thanks to pitcher **Justin Verlander**'s strong start. Boston bounced back, though, and won the next four games. Pitcher **David Price** had always struggled in the postseason. He did so again in Game 2, but the Sox won anyway! Boston OF **Jackie Bradley Jr.** had a grand slam to lead the way in Game 3. Game 4 ended with an 8–6 Boston win thanks to a spectacular diving catch in left field by **Andrew Benintendi**. If he had missed it, Houston probably would have won and evened the series. Price finally had a strong start in Game 5 and Boston clinched its first trip to the World Series since it won in 2013.

NLCS
Dodgers 4, Brewers 3

Los Angeles and Milwaukee split the first four games of this series. The Brewers knocked out Dodgers' ace Kershaw in Game 1 and put together a shutout to win Game 3. Meanwhile, LA depended on late magic. **Justin Turner**'s

Kershaw beat the Braves.

homer in the eighth inning clinched a Game 2 win, while **Cody Bellinger** delivered a walkoff single in the 13th inning of Game 4. Game 5 was a different story for Kershaw, as his seven-inning gem led the way to victory. Milwaukee tied the series again in Game 6. The clinching Game 7 went to LA thanks in part to a huge three-run homer by **Yasiel Puig**. The Dodgers headed to their second World Series in a row.

2018 World Series

Nuñez celebrated a huge homer.

Fenway Park. Sox starter **David Price** was awesome. He allowed only two runs in six innings. Boston OF **Andrew Benintendi** made a great running catch to save runs late in the game.

GAME 3: Dodgers 3, Red Sox 2

This one was epic. The headline in the *Los Angeles Times* after the game read "L.A. Marathon." The game took 7 hours and 20 minutes—and 18 innings—to play, setting World Series records in both categories. Fans and players and six very tired umpires watched as the two teams put up zero after zero. Boston's top four spots in the lineup wound up a combined 0-for-28! Every Red Sox player except for two pitchers appeared in the game. **Joc Pederson** homered in the third to give LA a 1–0 lead. Boston's **Jackie Bradley Jr.** smacked a longball that tied the score in the eighth. Both teams then scored in the 13th inning on errors! The *loooong*

GAME 1: Red Sox 8, Dodgers 4

With ace **Chris Sale** (Boston) and **Clayton Kershaw** (LA) on the mound, fans expected a pitcher's duel. Both teams brought their bats, though, and knocked the stars out early. Boston took advantage of a couple of LA mistakes, but the Dodgers came back to pull within 5–4. In the seventh, a big three-run, pinch-hit homer by Boston's **Eduardo Nuñez** sealed the win.

GAME 2: Red Sox 4, Dodgers 2

J. D. Martinez hit a two-run RBI single that broke open a close game as the Red Sox won two in a row at

Max Muncy ended a verrrry long game!

David can't put a Price on that smile!

night finally ended when LA's **Max Muncy** hit a walkoff homer in the bottom of the 18th inning.

GAME 4: Red Sox 9, Dodgers 6
The 2018 Dodgers were 54–0 when leading by four runs at any point in a game. LA went ahead 4–0 in the sixth inning on

a homer by **Yasiel Puig**. Boston, like LA still exhausted from the marathon Game 3, battled back, scoring nine runs in the final three innings. Pinch-hitter **Mitch Moreland** hit a three-run homer in the seventh. 1B **Steve Pearce** tied the game with a solo shot in the eighth. Pearce kept the ball rolling with a three-run double in Boston's five-run ninth inning. A ninth-inning Dodgers homer was not enough and Boston took a commanding lead in the Series.

GAME 5: Red Sox 5, Dodgers 1
Boston put this one away early. Pearce hit the sixth pitch Kershaw threw for a two-run homer. **Mookie Betts** and Martinez–and Pearce for a second time–added round-trippers later. Meanwhile, playoff hero Price returned to the mound and shut down the Dodgers again. He allowed a home run to the first batter, **David Freese**, but then only two hits over the next seven innings. Sale struck out Dodgers slugger **Manny Machado** for the final out. For the first time since 2013, and the fourth since 2004, the Boston Red Sox were World Series champions!

MVP! Boston 1B **Steve Pearce** was the easy choice for World Series MVP. His four RBIs in Game 4 broke open a vital game for Boston. In the clinching Game 5, he smacked a pair of homers! Pearce had only joined Boston in the summer after a trade with Toronto. He has now played for every team in the AL East, but remembers his time in Boston more than the others!

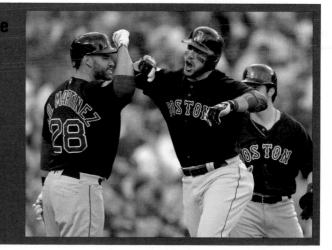

Stat Champs

AL Hitting Leaders

48 HR
Khris Davis, A's

130 RBI
J. D. Martinez, Red Sox

.346 BATTING AVERAGE
Mookie Betts, Red Sox

45 STOLEN BASES
192 HITS
Whit Merrifield, Royals

AL Pitching Leaders

21 WINS

1.89 ERA
Blake Snell, Rays

57 SAVES
Edwin Diaz, Mariners

290 STRIKEOUTS
Justin Verlander, Astros

NL Hitting Leaders

38 HOME RUNS
Nolan Arenado, Rockies

111 RBI
◀◀◀**Javier Baez**, Cubs

.326 BATTING AVERAGE
Christian Yelich, Brewers

191 HITS
Freddie Freeman, Braves

43 STOLEN BASES
Trea Turner, Nationals

NL Pitching Leaders

18 WINS
Jon Lester, Cubs
Miles Mikolas, Cardinals
Max Scherzer, Nationals

1.70 ERA
Jacob deGrom, Mets

300 STRIKEOUTS
Max Scherzer

43 SAVES
Wade Davis, Rockies

2018 Award Winners

MOST VALUABLE PLAYER
AL: **Mookie Betts**, RED SOX
NL: **Christian Yelich**, BREWERS

CY YOUNG AWARD
AL: **Blake Snell**, RAYS ▶▶▶
NL: **Jacob deGrom**, METS

ROOKIE OF THE YEAR
AL: **Shohei Ohtani**, ANGELS
NL: **Ronald Acuña**, BRAVES

MANAGER OF THE YEAR
AL: **Bob Melvin**, ATHLETICS
NL: **Brent Snitker**, BRAVES

HANK AARON AWARD (OFFENSE)
AL: **J. D. Martinez**, RED SOX
NL: **Christian Yelich**, BREWERS

ROBERTO CLEMENTE AWARD
(COMMUNITY SERVICE)
Yadier Molina, CARDINALS

Around the Bases 2019

Big Money!: Before the 2019 MLB season, several players made headlines as well as a LOT of money! First, **Manny Machado** signed a 10-year deal with the San Diego Padres that will pay him $300 million. The All-Star infielder is a rare combo of power and great defense. Soon after, **Bryce Harper** moved to the Philadelphia Phillies for $330 million. He'll earn that with his own all-around style for playing 13 seasons. Just before Harper signed, Gold Glove third baseman **Nolan Arenado** re-signed with Colorado. His deal for eight seasons pays an average of $32.5 million a season. In March, though, baseball's best player agreed to sign the biggest contract ever. The Angels will pay **Mike Trout** an incredible $430 million over 12 seasons. He'd better hit a lot of homers for all that!

Mike Trout

▲ **Mr. April:** Speaking of the Dodgers, LA's **Cody Bellinger** had the best April ever by a batter. He set MLB records for most RBI (37) and total bases (97) before the end of the season's first month. Bellinger and Milwaukee's **Christian Yelich** also tied the April record with 14 homers! Oh, and Bellinger ended the month leading the majors with a .431 average. Pretty good start!

Ouch: Through the end of May, an average of 0.41 batters per game had been hit by a pitch. Since 1900, that would be the highest mark ever (if it stayed that way through the full season).

What a Streak!

It's not baseball, it's softball, but it's worth a tip of the cap. The Oklahoma Sooners team set a new NCAA record by winning 41 games in a row. Ranked No. 1 for most of the season, they topped the old mark by two games. Coach **Patty Gasso** was okay with the streak ending. "We're happy that we don't have talk about this winning streak anymore. And we can just go about playing." Unfortunately for Sooners fans, they fell short of the NCAA title, losing in the Women's College World Series to UCLA.

Are pitchers getting worse? Or are hitters standing closer? Probably it's a little of both, as both sides try to get an advantage in baseball's most important battle.

Edwin Jackson

Booming Starts:

Once the games started, the Seattle Mariners made the biggest noise in the season's first month. The team's batters slugged at least one homer in each of Seattle's first 20 games. That's six better than the old Major League record. If you include homers from 2018, the Dodgers also set a record with 33 straight games with a homer. That included eight in their 2019 Opening Day win, which was another record!

◀◀◀On the Road Again:

Pitcher **Edwin Jackson** set an all-time record when he joined the Toronto Blue Jays. That moved his career total of different teams to 14, one more than **Octavio Dotel**'s 13. Here's the full list of Jackson's teams (in the order he played for them). Did he ever play for your favorite? If not, stick around—he'll probably be on the move again!

Dodgers, Rays, Tigers, Diamondbacks, White Sox, Cardinals, Nationals, Cubs, Braves, Padres, Marlins, Orioles, Athletics, Blue Jays.

World Series Winners

YEAR	WINNER	RUNNER-UP	SCORE*	YEAR	WINNER	RUNNER-UP	SCORE*
2018	Boston Red Sox	Los Angeles Dodgers	4-1	1990	Cincinnati Reds	Oakland Athletics	4-0
2017	Houston Astros	Los Angeles Dodgers	4-3	1989	Oakland Athletics	San Francisco Giants	4-0
2016	Chicago Cubs	Cleveland Indians	4-3	1988	Los Angeles Dodgers	Oakland Athletics	4-1
2015	Kansas City Royals	New York Mets	4-1	1987	Minnesota Twins	St. Louis Cardinals	4-3
2014	San Francisco Giants	Kansas City Royals	4-3	1986	New York Mets	Boston Red Sox	4-3
2013	Boston Red Sox	St. Louis Cardinals	4-2	1985	Kansas City Royals	St. Louis Cardinals	4-3
2012	San Francisco Giants	Detroit Tigers	4-0	1984	Detroit Tigers	San Diego Padres	4-1
2011	St. Louis Cardinals	Texas Rangers	4-3	1983	Baltimore Orioles	Philadelphia Phillies	4-1
2010	San Francisco Giants	Texas Rangers	4-1	1982	St. Louis Cardinals	Milwaukee Brewers	4-3
2009	New York Yankees	Philadelphia Phillies	4-2	1981	Los Angeles Dodgers	New York Yankees	4-2
2008	Philadelphia Phillies	Tampa Bay Rays	4-1	1980	Philadelphia Phillies	Kansas City Royals	4-2
2007	Boston Red Sox	Colorado Rockies	4-0	1979	Pittsburgh Pirates	Baltimore Orioles	4-3
2006	St. Louis Cardinals	Detroit Tigers	4-1	1978	New York Yankees	Los Angeles Dodgers	4-2
2005	Chicago White Sox	Houston Astros	4-0	1977	New York Yankees	Los Angeles Dodgers	4-2
2004	Boston Red Sox	St. Louis Cardinals	4-0	1976	Cincinnati Reds	New York Yankees	4-0
2003	Florida Marlins	New York Yankees	4-2	1975	Cincinnati Reds	Boston Red Sox	4-3
2002	Anaheim Angels	San Francisco Giants	4-3	1974	Oakland Athletics	Los Angeles Dodgers	4-1
2001	Arizona Diamondbacks	New York Yankees	4-3	1973	Oakland Athletics	New York Mets	4-3
2000	New York Yankees	New York Mets	4-1	1972	Oakland Athletics	Cincinnati Reds	4-3
1999	New York Yankees	Atlanta Braves	4-0	1971	Pittsburgh Pirates	Baltimore Orioles	4-3
1998	New York Yankees	San Diego Padres	4-0	1970	Baltimore Orioles	Cincinnati Reds	4-1
1997	Florida Marlins	Cleveland Indians	4-3	1969	New York Mets	Baltimore Orioles	4-1
1996	New York Yankees	Atlanta Braves	4-2	1968	Detroit Tigers	St. Louis Cardinals	4-3
1995	Atlanta Braves	Cleveland Indians	4-2	1967	St. Louis Cardinals	Boston Red Sox	4-3
1993	Toronto Blue Jays	Philadelphia Phillies	4-2	1966	Baltimore Orioles	Los Angeles Dodgers	4-0
1992	Toronto Blue Jays	Atlanta Braves	4-2	1965	Los Angeles Dodgers	Minnesota Twins	4-3
1991	Minnesota Twins	Atlanta Braves	4-3	1964	St. Louis Cardinals	New York Yankees	4-3

* Score is represented in games played.

YEAR	WINNER	RUNNER-UP	SCORE*	YEAR	WINNER	RUNNER-UP	SCORE*
1963	Los Angeles Dodgers	New York Yankees	4-0	1933	New York Giants	Washington Senators	4-1
1962	New York Yankees	San Francisco Giants	4-3	1932	New York Yankees	Chicago Cubs	4-0
1961	New York Yankees	Cincinnati Reds	4-1	1931	St. Louis Cardinals	Philadelphia Athletics	4-3
1960	Pittsburgh Pirates	New York Yankees	4-3	1930	Philadelphia Athletics	St. Louis Cardinals	4-2
1959	Los Angeles Dodgers	Chicago White Sox	4-2	1929	Philadelphia Athletics	Chicago Cubs	4-1
1958	New York Yankees	Milwaukee Braves	4-3	1928	New York Yankees	St. Louis Cardinals	4-0
1957	Milwaukee Braves	New York Yankees	4-3	1927	New York Yankees	Pittsburgh Pirates	4-0
1956	New York Yankees	Brooklyn Dodgers	4-3	1926	St. Louis Cardinals	New York Yankees	4-3
1955	Brooklyn Dodgers	New York Yankees	4-3	1925	Pittsburgh Pirates	Washington Senators	4-3
1954	New York Giants	Cleveland Indians	4-0	1924	Washington Senators	New York Giants	4-3
1953	New York Yankees	Brooklyn Dodgers	4-2	1923	New York Yankees	New York Giants	4-2
1952	New York Yankees	Brooklyn Dodgers	4-3	1922	New York Giants	New York Yankees	4-0
1951	New York Yankees	New York Giants	4-2	1921	New York Giants	New York Yankees	5-3
1950	New York Yankees	Philadelphia Phillies	4-0	1920	Cleveland Indians	Brooklyn Robins	5-2
1949	New York Yankees	Brooklyn Dodgers	4-1	1919	Cincinnati Reds	Chicago White Sox	5-3
1948	Cleveland Indians	Boston Braves	4-2	1918	Boston Red Sox	Chicago Cubs	4-2
1947	New York Yankees	Brooklyn Dodgers	4-3	1917	Chicago White Sox	New York Giants	4-2
1946	St. Louis Cardinals	Boston Red Sox	4-3	1916	Boston Red Sox	Brooklyn Robins	4-1
1945	Detroit Tigers	Chicago Cubs	4-3	1915	Boston Red Sox	Philadelphia Phillies	4-1
1944	St. Louis Cardinals	St. Louis Browns	4-2	1914	Boston Braves	Philadelphia Athletics	4-0
1943	New York Yankees	St. Louis Cardinals	4-1	1913	Philadelphia Athletics	New York Giants	4-1
1942	St. Louis Cardinals	New York Yankees	4-1	1912	Boston Red Sox	New York Giants	4-3
1941	New York Yankees	Brooklyn Dodgers	4-1	1911	Philadelphia Athletics	New York Giants	4-2
1940	Cincinnati Reds	Detroit Tigers	4-3	1910	Philadelphia Athletics	Chicago Cubs	4-1
1939	New York Yankees	Cincinnati Reds	4-0	1909	Pittsburgh Pirates	Detroit Tigers	4-3
1938	New York Yankees	Chicago Cubs	4-0	1908	Chicago Cubs	Detroit Tigers	4-1
1937	New York Yankees	New York Giants	4-1	1907	Chicago Cubs	Detroit Tigers	4-0
1936	New York Yankees	New York Giants	4-2	1906	Chicago White Sox	Chicago Cubs	4-2
1935	Detroit Tigers	Chicago Cubs	4-2	1905	New York Giants	Philadelphia Athletics	4-1
1934	St. Louis Cardinals	Detroit Tigers	4-3	1903	Boston Americans	Pittsburgh Pirates	5-3

Note: 1904 not played because NL-champion Giants refused to play; 1994 not played due to MLB work stoppage.

SOCCER

CHAMPIONS!

Succeeding under pressure is one of the hardest things in sports. In the summer of 2019, the American women's national soccer team did that and more. Facing the toughest teams in the world, and watched closely by millions, the US women came through in the clutch. They earned their fourth World Cup championship with a 2–0 win over the Netherlands. Kelley O'Hara, Alex Morgan, and Allie Long show how much they loved winning!

Vive le Soccer!

Long live soccer indeed! France put on a fantastic World Cup, as fans packed stadiums all over the country for the Women's World Cup.

The action on the pitch gave all those fans a great show. European teams dominated play in the early rounds. Seven of the eight teams in the quarterfinals were from that continent.

Italy was one of the surprise teams. Playing in their first World Cup, they defeated Australia and later beat China. The Netherlands came in as the European champion, but they were still an underdog. The Dutch showed why they were champs, though, and made it to the final. England put on a great show, featuring the goal-scoring wizard **Ellen White**, who had six in her team's games. African countries also did better than ever, as both Cameroon and Nigeria made it into the Round of 16. Jamaica also made its first-ever World Cup.

The American team came in as the defending champions and showed right away that they were ready to protect their title. They romped through the early rounds, piling on the goals while also putting up a solid wall of defense. Still, as the knockout rounds continued, it became clear that the US was not alone as a great women's soccer nation anymore.

The great play of many teams showed that the women's game is definitely on the rise. Read on to follow all the action!

One of the surprise teams was Italy (in blue). The Italians upset powerful Australia (yellow).

First-Round Action

Great Start for Europe

All of the WWC teams from that continent won their opening games, except for Scotland. The biggest win was for Italy. They were making their Women's World Cup debut but beat favored Australia 2–1.

Just in Time

New Zealand almost came up with a shocking 0–0 tie against No. 8 Netherlands. In stoppage time, though, **Jill Roord** nodded in a goal to let the Orange squeak through with a 1–0 win.

Koala Komeback!

In its second Group C game against Brazil, Australia became the second team ever to overcome a 2–0 goal deficit to win in the WWC. The Matildas gave up an early penalty, which was scored by the great **Marta**. **Cristiane** scored on a header to make it 2–0 Brazil. An Australian goal late in the half and another early in the second tied the game. Brazil then allowed an own goal in the 66th minute, and Australia held on for the win. In the Aussies' third game, **Samantha Kerr** scored four goals to tie **Alex Morgan** for the tournament lead.

Ajara Nchout of Cameroon

Awesome Africans

For the first time, two countries from Africa made it into the Round of 16. Nigeria squeaked in after Chile failed to score three goals in its final game. Cameroon made it by beating New Zealand. **Ajara Nchout** scored in the fifth minute of added time to pull the upset.

Round of 16 News

* Norway knocked out Australia and superstar Kerr on penalties, 4–1.

* Europe continued to dominate. Seven of the eight quarterfinal spots went to teams from that continent.

American Action

Rapinoe's penalties helped beat Spain.

USA 13, Thailand 0

The United States began its defense of its 2015 World Cup with a huge victory. Seven players scored as the Americans romped. Striker **Alex Morgan** had five by herself! The team's 13 goals set an all-time World Cup record for goals in a game—by men's or women's teams! Some people thought the US should have let up late in the game. The players, though, knew that their goal total was important in the group standings.

USA 3, Chile 0

In the second US game, coach **Jill Ellis** showed off her team's deep roster. She swapped in seven new players. The Americans still won, beating Chile 3–0. **Carli Lloyd** scored two goals. She became the first player ever to score in six straight World Cup games. **Tierna Davidson** had two assists and became the youngest US World Cup player since 1995 at 20 years old.

USA 2, Sweden 0

The Swedes proved to be a tougher challenge for the US, but the Americans made it three wins in a row and won their group. It was a fast-moving game. Sweden challenged goalie **Alyssa Naeher**, but she was up to it, making three saves. **Lindsey Horan** scored in the third minute. **Tobin Heath** bounced in a goal off a Swedish player later in the first half. Next stop: The Round of 16!

ROUND OF 16:
USA 2, Spain 1

The US team gave up its first goal of the tournament after a bad pass in the back. They kept up the pressure, though, and earned two penalties. Veteran **Megan Rapinoe** buried both and the Americans survived a tough match.

Quarterfinals

USA 2, France 1
In the biggest game of the tournament so far, the Americans held off a tough French team in front of a huge home crowd. **Megan Rapinoe** scored on a free kick in the fourth minute. She doubled the lead in the second half. After a late French header by **Wendie Renard**, the US buckled down to stop a French comeback.

England 3, Norway 0
The Lionesses continued their strong World Cup performance with a dominating win. Superstar **Lucy Bronze** smacked in a great long-distance goal while also helping with assists on goals by **Ellen White** and **Jill Scott**. White moved into a three-way tie for the Golden Boot award for most goals.

Netherlands 2, Italy 0
Italy's surprising run ended when the Dutch team shut them out. The Netherlands used their heads to win. They got head-ball goals in the second half from **Vivianne Miedema** and **Stefanie van der Gragt**. The win sent the Netherlands to its first-ever Women's World Cup semifinal.

Sweden 2, Germany 1
The Swedes shocked the favored German team to advance to the semifinals. Germany was also knocked out of the 2020 Olympics; where teams finish at the World Cup determines who qualifies for the Games. The game was tied 1-1 in the second half when **Sofia Jakobsson** rammed home the game-winner. It was the first quarterfinal comeback win by any team in 20 years.

Lucy Bronze (2) cracked in this long shot to help England advance past Norway.

Dutch soccer took a huge leap forward when their team beat Sweden.

WWC Semifinals

USA 2, ENGLAND 1

This game began with a shock: **Megan Rapinoe** was not in the lineup. American fans worried that the team would be hurt without their scoring star. Her replacement **Christen Press**, however, scored on a header in the first half. No more worries! Still, England gave the Americans a tough fight and tied the score on a goal by **Ellen White**. Then in the 31st minute, **Alex Morgan** knocked in a header of her own. That gave her the lead in the race for the Golden Boot, given to the player who scores the most World Cup goals. Goalie **Alyssa Naeher** ssa Naeher stopped a second-half penalty shot. The Americans returned to the final!

NETHERLANDS 1, SWEDEN 0

For the first time ever, a Women's World Cup semifinal needed extra time. No one scored for the first 90 minutes as these top European teams battled. Sweden's goalie **Hedvig Lindahl** kept her team in the game with key saves. Not long after extra time began, in the 99th minute, **Jackie Groenen** scored the game's only goal and the Dutch team held on for the win. Not bad for a country that actually banned women from playing soccer until the early 1970s! The victory sent the Netherlands to its first-ever Women's World Cup final.

USA! USA! USA!

The World Cup final matched America and the Netherlands. For the first time in the World Cup, the American team did not score in the first 15 minutes. For the first time, they were held scoreless by halftime. For the first time, they faced a goalie who was knocking away every shot they took. Were the Americans worried? Heck no!

Playing in its record third straight World Cup final, the US team did what everyone expected it to do—face down every challenge and win. **Alex Morgan** earned a penalty kick in the 61st minute. **Megan Rapinoe** smacked it home for her sixth World Cup goal.

Eight minutes later, **Rose Lavelle** snaked past two Dutch defenders. She smashed a left-footed shot past a diving goalie for her third goal in the Cup.

That was all the American team needed. Their defense buckled down and prevented any chance of a comeback. As the final whistle blew, the 23 members of the team poured onto the pitch to dance, celebrate, and cry. America becomes the first country since Germany to win back-to-back World Cups and the first ever with four titles. The team scored 26 goals in all, another all-time record.

Let the celebration begin!

WOMEN'S WORLD AWARDS

(BEST PLAYERS)

GOLDEN BALL
Megan Rapinoe, US

SILVER BALL
Lucy Bronze, England

BRONZE BALL
Rose Lavelle, US

GOLDEN BOOT (TOP SCORER)
Megan Rapinoe, US

GOLDEN GLOVES (BEST GOALIE)
Sari van Veenendaal,
Netherlands

Megan Rapinoe

FIFA Women's World Cup France 2019™

MLS 2018

Martínez set a record and won a Cup.

The 2018 MLS season featured a new scoring champ and a new attention-grabbing champ! Atlanta United forward **Josef Martínez** scored 31 goals, breaking the old record of 27. In Los Angeles, Swedish star **Zlatan Ibrahimović** thrilled Galaxy fans with a series of highlight-reel goals. He scored one from more than 40 yards, looping it over the goalie's head. He karate-kicked a volley for his 500th career goal (not all in MLS, of course).

Wayne Rooney, the former England star, played a big role with DC United. He was probably the league MVP of the second half, scoring 12 goals and seven assists while leading his team to the playoffs.

Atlanta had a chance for best regular-season record, but lost its last game to Toronto. Meanwhile, the New York Red Bulls beat Orlando on the last weekend to capture the Supporters' Shield for third time. New York's 71 total points set a new MLS record as well.

Out West, LAFC was the big story. They had the best record ever for a first-year team and the third-best record in MLS in 2018.

Conference Championship Games

In the Eastern Conference final, Atlanta continued its amazing season and the Red Bulls were disappointed again. Three times in the past six seasons, the New York–based team has had the top record in MLS, and they've played in five conference finals. With all that success, the top spot has eluded them. Atlanta made sure it happened again, winning 3–1 in the two-game final.

In the West, Portland shocked Sporting Kansas City. After a scoreless tie in the first leg in Portland, the Timber won at Sporting's home 3–2. A fantastic long-range goal by **Sebastian Blanco** tied the score and silenced the home crowd. The first of two goals by **Diego Valeri** clinched Portland's conference title.

MLS CUP 2018

In front of an MLS Cup record 73,000 fans, Atlanta United capped off its amazing second season with a league championship. Record-setting goal-scorer **Josef Martínez** dribbled around the keeper to score first. **Franco Escobar** added a second goal off a corner kick for the 2–0 final. Portland could not handle the Atlanta offense and the super-loud crowd. It was the first pro sports championship for Atlanta since the Braves won the 1995 World Series.

NWSL

In a rematch of the 2017 National Women's Soccer League championship game, the North Carolina Courage got revenge. They beat the Portland Thorns 3–0 to win the 2018 title. Portland had won that 2017 game. The Courage's Jess McDonald scored twice in the title game. It was not a big surprise win. North Carolina had only lost once in the regular season, setting NWSL records with 17 wins, 57 points, and 58 goals.

The good news for the league was that the championship game set a new attendance record for a women's pro soccer game in the US. The

21,144 fans who watched in Portland were also sure to enjoy the 2019 Women's World Cup that was played in June (see page 60). The Courage faced an additional hurdle. Hurricane Florence forced the team to play its earlier playoff game on the road before facing the Thorns on their home field. But North Carolina clearly had all the "courage" it needed to win!

World Soccer Highlights

A New Best Player

For ten years, the award for best male player in the world went to just two players: **Cristiano Ronaldo** and **Lionel Messi**. Their streak of taking turns winning the "Best" trophy ended in 2018. Midfielder **Luka Modrić** (right) of Real Madrid and Croatia took home the award afer helping his club team win the Champions League and leading his national team to a runner-up finish at the World Cup. **Ada Hegerberg** of Norway was named the women's winner.

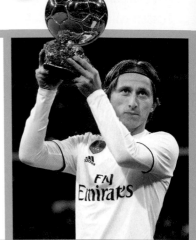

UEFA Nations League

The international championship of European countries is played every four years. The next tournament will be in 2020. In years when the event is not held, national teams used to play "friendlies." In 2019, they made things more intersting, creating the new Nations League. This time, the games counted and more top players took part. A total of 55 countries entered. They were split into four "leagues," ranked by overall success. After the games were all played, the top four teams in League A made the semifinals. Portugal beat Switzerland in one semi, while the Netherlands beat England. The final was in Porto, Portugal, and the home side won. **Gonçalo Guedes** scored the only goal of the game, giving Portuguese superstar **Cristiano Ronaldo** (left) another trophy for his huge collection.

Lucas Moura's goal capped off an incredible comeback by Tottenham Hotspur.

UEFA CHAMPIONS LEAGUE

The biggest prize in pro soccer is the UEFA Champions League (UCL). The top teams from all the major pro leagues in Europe spend nearly a year battling through a series of matches. Among the 2019 early-round highlights was a hat trick from **Cristiano Ronaldo**. He led his Juventus team back from a 2–0 loss to Atletico Madrid. Paris St.-Germain was surprised to go home after losing to the reserve squad from Manchester United. Liverpool pulled off a big upset over Bayern Munich to advance.

In the second legs of the total-goal semifinals, fans watched two of the most amazing UCL games ever played.

After its first matchup, Liverpool trailed 3–0 to powerful FC Barcelona, led by **Lionel Messi**. In the second game, the English club got one goal back after seven minutes. They then shocked the Spaniards by scoring three more goals in the second half. The series-winning goal came in the 80th minute from **Divock Origi**. He banged home a shot off a "quick" corner kick that caught the Spanish team napping. It was one of the biggest comebacks in UCL history.

The second semifinal was even wilder. Tottenham Hotspur trailed Ajax 1–0 after the first leg. In the second, the 'Spurs gave up two more goals and trailed 3–0 at halftime. Tottenham battled back with two goals by **Lucas Moura**. Ajax was set to advance but with less than a minute left, Moura smacked in his third goal of the game to set off a wild celebration.

The all-English final ended with Liverpool winning its seventh Champions League title, as they beat Tottenham 1–0.

Stat Stuff

MLS CHAMPIONS

2018	Atlanta United
2017	Toronto FC
2016	Seattle Sounders
2015	Portland Timbers
2014	LA Galaxy
2013	Sporting Kansas City
2012	LA Galaxy
2011	LA Galaxy
2010	Colorado Rapids
2009	Real Salt Lake
2008	Columbus Crew
2007	Houston Dynamo
2006	Houston Dynamo
2005	LA Galaxy
2004	D.C. United
2003	San Jose Earthquakes
2002	LA Galaxy
2001	San Jose Earthquakes
2000	Kansas City Wizards
1999	D.C. United
1998	Chicago Fire
1997	D.C. United
1996	D.C. United

UEFA CHAMPIONS LEAGUE

The top club teams from the members of UEFA (the Union of European Football Associations) face off in this months-long tournament.

2019	Liverpool FC	ENGLAND
2018	Real Madrid	SPAIN
2017	Real Madrid	SPAIN
2016	Real Madrid	SPAIN
2015	FC Barcelona	SPAIN
2014	Real Madrid	SPAIN
2013	Bayern Munich	GERMANY
2012	Chelsea FC	ENGLAND
2011	FC Barcelona	SPAIN
2010	Inter Milan	ITALY
2009	FC Barcelona	SPAIN
2008	Manchester United	ENGLAND
2007	AC Milan	ITALY
2006	FC Barcelona	SPAIN
2005	Liverpool FC	ENGLAND
2004	FC Porto	PORTUGAL
2003	AC Milan	ITALY
2002	Real Madrid	SPAIN

WOMEN'S WORLD CUP WINNERS

YEAR	CHAMPION	RUNNER-UP
2019	**USA**	Netherlands
2015	**USA**	Japan
2011	**Japan**	USA
2007	**Germany**	Brazil
2003	**Germany**	Sweden
1999	**USA**	China
1995	**Norway**	Germany
1991	**USA**	Norway

GOLDEN BALL WINNERS

2019	**MEGAN RAPINOE**, USA
2015	**CARLI LLOYD**, USA
2011	**HOMARE SAWA**, Japan
2007	**MARTA**, Brazil
2003	**BIRGIT PRINZ**, Germany
1999	**SUN WEN**, China
1995	**HEGE RIISE**, Norway
1991	**CARIN JENNINGS**, USA

NUMBERS, NUMBERS

Duke superstar Zion Williamson wore number 1 and was the number-one story in college basketball in 2018–19. Then he was the number-one NBA Draft pick. Williamson did not get to hold up a No. 1 at the end of the season, however. To find out who did, read on!

COLLEGE BASKETBALL

Surprise Ending!

Zion, Zion, Zion! It seemed like the 2018–19 men's college basketball season was all about one player: Duke freshman **Zion Williamson**. He was certainly worth watching! The powerful 6'7" forward created highlights in just about every game he played. He could soar to the hoop for dunks or fly high for blocks. He helped Duke stay near number one most of the season. One of the year's most memorable moments came early in a big game against North Carolina. As Williamson made a cut, his sneaker tore open! His foot slipped out and he twisted his knee. Former president **Barack Obama** was among the many celebrities at this big event, which was suddenly without its biggest star! After missing several games, Williamson returned to cheers and led Duke to the Elite Eight.

And that's when the surprises happened! In the Elite Eight game against Michigan State, Williamson

and Duke were upset. All four of the games in that round were classic, super-tight contests that thrilled fans. In the end, only one team seeded No. 1 in the NCAA tournament made the Final Four. To find out how that turned out, check out page 87!

College hoops had other big stories this season. Gonzaga used a veteran group of players to storm to the top of the regular-season rankings. Tennessee played great defense and returned to a place among the top teams. Like Duke, Kentucky relied on a group of freshmen. Most headed to the NBA in 2019, but they gave Wildcats fans a very solid season.

Women's college basketball went a bit more as expected. A handful of superteams continued to dominate the rankings. At the Final Four, it was a battle of titans, as some of the most successful schools in the sport's history took each other on. Only one could come out on top, though. Find out more starting on page 88.

Kentucky's Keldon Johnson

AWARD WINNERS

NAISMITH AWARDS
Zion Williamson/DUKE
Megan Gustafson/IOWA

WOODEN AWARD
Zion Williamson/DUKE
Sabrina Ionescu/OREGON

AP COACH OF THE YEAR
Chris Beard/TEXAS TECH
Kim Mulkey/BAYLOR

Megan Gustafson of Iowa

FINAL MEN'S TOP 10
Associated Press
1. Virginia
2. Texas Tech
3. Michigan State
4. Duke
5. Auburn
6. Gonzaga
7. Kentucky
8. Purdue
9. North Carolina
10. Tennessee

FINAL WOMEN'S TOP 10
USA Today Coaches Poll
1. Baylor
2. Notre Dame
3. Connecticut
4. Oregon
5. Mississippi State
6. Louisville
7. Stanford
8. Iowa
9. North Carolina State
10. Oregon State

Hoops! 2018-19

Arizona State shocked the Kansas Jayhawks.

Not Very 'Nova: Villanova was the defending champion and had also won back in 2016. Early in the 2018–19 season, though, the Wildcats were swamped 73–46 in a title-game rematch with Michigan. Then 'Nova lost to unranked Furman. Not a good start for the champs!

Aloha, No. 1: Gonzaga came into the season with high hopes and a seasoned team. But the Bulldogs needed a big win to jump in the rankings. They got it during an early season tournament in Hawaii. The 'Zags beat No. 1 Duke 89–87 and moved into the No. 1 spot in the rankings! Then, in December, Kansas had taken over the top

259,984

That's how many three-point shots NCAA men's players heaved up in 2018-19. That set a new all-time record. They made 89,821 of them, which was another record. Some people were saying that the NCAA should consider moving the three-point line back. What do you think?

Grant Williams was perfect for Tennessee.

drained a three-point shot at the buzzer to give the Utes an amazing 93–92 win.

Super Shot: With the final seconds ticking down in a Missouri State-Illinois State game, a football game broke out. A pile of players tried to grab the ball near midcourt. It finally bounced to **Jarred Dixon** of Missouri State. He heaved up a half-court shot that banked in to give his football, er, basketball team a stunning 66–65 win!

Tournament Surprises:

No. 1 Gonzaga had just one more hurdle to leap before the NCAA tournament began. It had to beat unranked St. Mary's in the West Coast Conference tournament final.
St. Mary's shocked the Bulldogs with a 60–47 win! The Gaels played awesome defense and ended Gonzaga's 21-game winning streak. Bad news for the 'Zags: The women's team was also upset in the WCC final by Brigham Young!

spot. The Jayhawks lost it after being upset by Arizona State 80–78. ASU was behind by seven, but ended the game with a 13–2 run for the big win.

Wildcat Woes: Kentucky was

charging up the rankings in December and had reached No. 9. The team didn't stay there long. Unranked Seton Hall pulled off an early season upset. The Pirates beat the Wildcats 84–83.

Perfect: In a January overtime win

over Vanderbilt, **Grant Williams** of Tennessee led the way with 43 points. He got 23 of them from the free-throw line . . . in 23 attempts! Williams's perfect night was the second-best in NCAA history. Oklahoma State's **Arlen Clark** went 24-for-24 way back in 1959!

Comeback!: With about 12

minutes left in the UCLA-Utah game, some fans probably left. UCLA led by 22 points! The fans that stuck around saw their Bruins have a miserable meltdown. UCLA got very cold and Utah got super hot. The Utes scored a total of 61 points . . . in the second half alone! Utah's **Parker Van Dyke**

Parker Van Dyke of Utah celebrates his winning shot.

Tournament Time: Men

Texas Tech upset Michigan State.

GO ANTEATERS!: No. 13 UC Irvine earned the first NCAA tournament victory in school history with a surprising 70–64 win over Kansas State.

CLOSE CALL: Remember UMBC? In 2018, the Retrievers became the first No. 16 ever to beat a No. 1. Iona must have watched that game. The Gaels led No. 1 North Carolina at halftime of their opening-round game. However, the Tar Heels were not about to allow a repeat and turned it around for an 88–73 win.

COMEBACK: Tennessee trailed by as many as 18 points in the second half against Purdue. The Vols rallied to force overtime and escaped with a 99–94 win.

RECORD SETTER: As Wofford beat Seton Hall 84–68, Fletcher Magee made seven three-pointers. That made him the NCAA all-time leader in "treys" with 509.

IT'S ALWAYS THE 12S: Every year, fans look for the upset in the No. 5 versus No. 12 games. They just always seem to happen! The 2019 tournament was no different. Three No. 12s won. Oregon beat Wisconsin, Murray State shocked Marquette, and Liberty beat Mississippi State. Only No. 5 Auburn escaped the No. 12 jinx, and the Tigers went on to make the Final Four!

GOODBYE, WOLVERINES!: The biggest surprise in the round of 16 was No. 3 Texas Tech's big win over No. 2 Michigan. The Red Raiders had never made a Final Four, while Michigan had been to nine. Tech swamped the Wolverines with tight defense and won 64–44.

VERY ELITE EIGHT

All four of the Elite Eight games were terrific. No. 1 Virginia needed overtime (after a buzzer-beating shot to tie in regulation) to beat No. 3 Purdue 80–75. Texas Tech shocked No. 1 Gonzaga 75–69 in a great, fast-paced game. No. 2 Michigan State ended **Zion Williamson**'s season early as the Spartans held on to beat top-seeded Duke 68–67. Finally, Auburn went to overtime *(left)* to hold off Kentucky 77–71.

Cavs Are the Champs!

The national semifinals produced an upset and a controversy. Texas Tech surprised favored Michigan State 61–51 to advance to the Red Raiders' first national final. Virginia squeaked by Auburn 63–62. The winning points came on three free throws awarded to **Kyle Guy** after a foul call with 0.6 seconds left (and after a double-dribble call against Virginia was missed with four seconds left). Guy calmly made all three and sent the Cavaliers to a showdown with Tech.

In the final, one thing was sure: One team would win its first-ever national championship. Defense was expected to be the big story. Both teams were in the top three in the nation in scoring defense. Virginia and Texas Tech were just too good, however. They both hit clutch shots over and over. Virginia led by 10 at one point, but Tech rallied to take a late lead. Then Virginia hit a three-pointer with 12 seconds left to tie the game 68–68. For the first time since 2008, the final went to overtime! In OT, Virginia rolled. The Cavaliers made 12 straight free throws and kept Tech from scoring very much. Virginia celebrated its 85–77 victory with golden confetti!

NCAA Women 2018–19

As usual in women's hoops, a few top teams dominated the headlines. However, most of the key schools faced big challenges as they stormed toward the Final Four. First to fall was Connecticut, by far the best school in women's basketball history. Baylor snapped the Huskies' amazing streak of 126 regular-season wins in a row in a January upset. UConn had not lost outside of the NCAA tournament since 2014!

Showdowns between top teams continued. Later in January, No. 1 Notre Dame faced No. 2 Louisville. It was a close game until late, as Louisville closed to within two points. Then Irish star **Arike Ogunbowale** started nailing threes, and the Cardinals faded. Near the end of the month, however, Notre Dame was on the other end of the story. North Carolina stunned the Fighting Irish with a 78–73 victory. How much of a surprise was this? It was the first time in 198 games—and only the fourth time ever—that an unranked team had beaten a No. 1 team!

The NCAA tournament held a few surprises, but ended with a familiar team on top. Read on!

Record Setter

Sabrina Ionescu became college basketball's all-time triple-double leader. With her 13th career game with double-figures in points, rebounds, and assists, she broke the career record set by men's player Kyle Collinsworth. Ionescu had eight of those games in the 2018–19 season, setting a single-season record, too! Her all-around game helped Oregon reach the Final Four in the NCAA tournament.

Tournament Time: Women

Oregon State was part of a solid Pac-12.

the Sweet 16. The Lady Bears earned the right to play there (and lose to No. 2 Stanford) by beating No. 6 DePaul and No. 3 Iowa State.

Big Pac: The Pac-12 men's teams struggled in the 2019 tournament. Only Oregon survived two games. In the women's bracket, though, the Pac-12 soared. Five of the Sweet 16 teams came from the conference: Oregon, Stanford, UCLA, Oregon State, and Arizona State.

Welcome to 16: No. 6 South
Dakota State beat No. 11 Quinnipiac in the first round. Then the Jackrabbits had to face No. 3 Syracuse on the Orange's home court! They ignored the crowd and claimed a 75–64 win. Madison Guebert scored 20 points as South Dakota State headed to its first-ever Sweet 16.

Surprise 16: No. 11 Missouri State
was the only team seeded lower than sixth in

South Dakota State (yellow) upset Syracuse.

NCAA Women's Semifinals

Notre Dame rallied to make the final.

NOTRE DAME 81, CONNECTICUT 76

Trailing by nine in the final quarter, Notre Dame needed a spark. They got it from a familiar player: Arike Ogunbowale. The hero of the team's 2018 title run poured in 14 points in the fourth. That gave her 23 and more than enough to beat Connecticut. The Irish earned a chance to become the first repeat NCAA champ since . . . Connecticut in 2016!

BAYLOR 72, OREGON 67

Sometimes having experience really makes the difference. Oregon was in its first national semifinal. Baylor was playing in its fourth! Oregon did its best, keeping the game tight until the final quarter. Then the Ducks went cold. They missed 12 of their final 13 shots. Baylor kept up the pressure. The Bears headed to a showdown with Notre Dame seeking the school's third NCAA title.

Kalani Brown (with trophy) and her Baylor teammates celebrate a title amid the confetti!

Baylor Wins!
NATIONAL CHAMPIONSHIP

Whew! That's what the Baylor Bears were thinking as the final shot of the women's national championship game went in. It was a free throw by Notre Dame star **Arike Ogunbowale**. The one point basket was not enough, however. She had missed the previous shot. So as the final shot went in, Notre Dame was one point short, and Baylor was the 2019 champion with a dramatic 82–81 victory.

For most of the game, it did not look like Baylor would have to sweat out a close finish. The Bears' defense shut down Notre Dame for most of three quarters. Baylor led by 12 points at halftime and again late in the third quarter. Then star center **Lauren Cox** went out with a knee injury. Notre Dame rallied for the lead with less than five minutes left. Both teams had chances to put the game away late, but Baylor took the last lead on a layup by **Chloe Jackson** with 3.9 seconds remaining.

Ogunbowale was fouled with 1.9 seconds left, preventing her from making a tying shot. Sent to the line, she needed to make both free throws. Irish fans were shocked when she missed the first. As she tried to miss the second and earn a possible rebound, the ball went in! Baylor earned its third national title, its first since 2012.

NCAA Champs!

MEN'S DIVISION I

2019 Virginia	2000 Michigan State	1981 Indiana
2018 Villanova	1999 Connecticut	1980 Louisville
2017 North Carolina	1998 Kentucky	1979 Michigan State
2016 Villanova	1997 Arizona	1978 Kentucky
2015 Duke	1996 Kentucky	1977 Marquette
2014 Connecticut	1995 UCLA	1976 Indiana
2013 Louisville	1994 Arkansas	1975 UCLA
2012 Kentucky	1993 North Carolina	1974 NC State
2011 Connecticut	1992 Duke	1973 UCLA
2010 Duke	1991 Duke	1972 UCLA
2009 North Carolina	1990 UNLV	1971 UCLA
2008 Kansas	1989 Michigan	1970 UCLA
2007 Florida	1988 Kansas	1969 UCLA
2006 Florida	1987 Indiana	1968 UCLA
2005 North Carolina	1986 Louisville	1967 UCLA
2004 Connecticut	1985 Villanova	1966 Texas Western
2003 Syracuse	1984 Georgetown	1965 UCLA
2002 Maryland	1983 NC State	1964 UCLA
2001 Duke	1982 North Carolina	1963 Loyola (Illinois)

1962 **Cincinnati**	1954 **La Salle**	1946 **Oklahoma A&M**
1961 **Cincinnati**	1953 **Indiana**	1945 **Oklahoma A&M**
1960 **Ohio State**	1952 **Kansas**	1944 **Utah**
1959 **California**	1951 **Kentucky**	1943 **Wyoming**
1958 **Kentucky**	1950 **City Coll. of NY**	1942 **Stanford**
1957 **North Carolina**	1949 **Kentucky**	1941 **Wisconsin**
1956 **San Francisco**	1948 **Kentucky**	1940 **Indiana**
1955 **San Francisco**	1947 **Holy Cross**	1939 **Oregon**

WOMEN'S DIVISION I

2019 **Baylor**	2006 **Maryland**	1993 **Texas Tech**
2018 **Notre Dame**	2005 **Baylor**	1992 **Stanford**
2017 **South Carolina**	2004 **Connecticut**	1991 **Tennessee**
2016 **Connecticut**	2003 **Connecticut**	1990 **Stanford**
2015 **Connecticut**	2002 **Connecticut**	1989 **Tennessee**
2014 **Connecticut**	2001 **Notre Dame**	1988 **Louisiana Tech**
2013 **Connecticut**	2000 **Connecticut**	1987 **Tennessee**
2012 **Baylor**	1999 **Purdue**	1986 **Texas**
2011 **Texas A&M**	1998 **Tennessee**	1985 **Old Dominion**
2010 **Connecticut**	1997 **Tennessee**	1984 **USC**
2009 **Connecticut**	1996 **Tennessee**	1983 **USC**
2008 **Tennessee**	1995 **Connecticut**	1982 **Louisiana Tech**
2007 **Tennessee**	1994 **North Carolina**	

WNBA/NBA

O CANADA!
Fans in Toronto posed for NBA Finals MVP Kawhi Leonard for a really, really big selfie. The hometown Raptors became the first Canadian team to win the league title. They knocked off the defending champion Golden State Warriors in five games. For all the details of the WNBA and NBA seasons, keep dribbling . . . er, reading!

2018 WNBA

The WNBA continued to grow in popularity in 2018. New young stars joined the vets as records fell and attendance grew! The league continued into 2019 as one of the fastest-rising pro sports in the country. Here's a look back at the best of 2018.

Bird is the WNBA games played champ.

Pouring in Points from Down Under

On July 17, **Liz Cambage** wrote a new page in the WNBA record book. The 6-8 center from Australia poured in 53 points for the Dallas Wings, who beat the New York Liberty 104–87. Cambage was 17 out of 22 in shooting, and she missed only one of her 16 free-throw attempts. As if that was not enough, Cambage had 35 points the next game. Not surprisingly, that was a new two-game WNBA record! (Cambage moved to the Las Vegas Aces for the 2019 season.)

Triple the Fun!

Triple-doubles are a rare thing in the WNBA, so when a player gets double digits in three stat categories in one game, it's news. In a July 20 victory by the Chicago Sky over the Dallas Wings, all-star guard **Courtney Vandersloot** was the newsmaker. She became the seventh WNBA player with a triple-double in a single game. Vandersloot scored 13 points and had 10 rebounds and 15 assists.

WNBA AWARDS WINNERS

MVP: **Breanna Stewart**, Seattle
DEFENSIVE PLAYER OF THE YEAR: **Alana Beard**, Los Angeles
ROOKIE OF THE YEAR: **A'ja Wilson**, Las Vegas
MOST IMPROVED PLAYER: **Natasha Howard**, Seattle
SIXTH WOMAN OF THE YEAR: **Jonquel Jones**, Connecticut
COACH OF THE YEAR: **Nicki Collen**, Atlanta

A Season of Records

WNBA record-keepers were very busy as several athletes hit major milestones in 2018.

* **Sue Bird** became the WNBA all-time leader in games played on July 22. When Bird took the court for the Seattle Storm against the Atlanta Dream, it was her 500th game, topping **DeLisha Milton-Jones**'s 499 career games. Bird ended the regular season with 508 WNBA games played.

* Scoring machine **Diana Taurasi** became the first WNBA player to top 8,000 career points.

* The league also got a new all-time rebounding leader. In a July 5 win over the Sparks, Minnesota's **Rebekkah Brunson** moved from third to first all-time in rebounds. She ended the season with a new record 3,356 boards.

* **Shekinna Stricklen** tied a single-game record with 8 three-pointers. Her 24 points led the way for a Sun victory over the Wings.

2018 STANDINGS*

EASTERN CONFERENCE

Atlanta Dream	23-11
Washington Mystics	22-12
Connecticut Sun	21-13
Chicago Sky	13-21
New York Liberty	7-27
Indiana Fever	6-28

WESTERN CONFERENCE

Seattle Storm	26-8
Phoenix Mercury	20-14
Los Angeles Sparks	19-15
Minnesota Lynx	18-16
Dallas Wings	15-19
Las Vegas Aces	14-20

* Regular-Season

A'ja Wilson was the WNBA Rookie of the Year.

2018 WNBA Playoffs

Bird and Griner played an epic semifinals.

> **"***That was some of the best basketball that I've ever seen in the WNBA.***"**
> — SEATTLE STORM COACH **DAN HUGHES** AFTER GAME 5

More teams than ever made it into the WNBA playoffs, but some of them didn't stay very long. The league added two pairs of one-game playoffs that sent the winners to the conference semifinals, where higher-seeded teams waited.

First Round

Phoenix 101–Dallas 83
Los Angeles 75–Minnesota 68

The Mercury earned another game for veteran star **Diana Taurasi**. The other game was a rematch of the 2017 WNBA Finals. Defending champ Minnesota was sent home early.

Second Round

Phoenix 96–Connecticut 86
Washington 96–Los Angeles 64

Phoenix continued its great late-season run, surprising higher-seeded Connecticut. The Mystics whomped the Sparks; it was the biggest loss by points in Sparks playoff history.

Conference Semifinals

Seattle over Phoenix

The Storm were the story of the 2018 season, finishing with the best overall record and rolling through most opponents. They opened this series with two quick victories, but Phoenix did not give up. Led by star center **Brittney Griner**, the Mercury rallied to win the next two games and force a deciding Game 5. It proved to be epic. The two teams went back-and-forth in Seattle, with each holding the lead. WNBA MVP **Breanna Stewart** was a difference-maker. She scored 28 points while defending Griner. In the fourth quarter, **Sue Bird** scored 14 points despite wearing a mask to protect a broken nose. Seattle won 94–84.

Washington over Atlanta

The favored Dream won two of the first three games. But the Mystics responded with a 21-point victory in Game 4 and won Game 5 on the road, 86–81, led by **Ariel Atkins**'s 20 points and **Elena Delle Donne**'s 14 points and 11 rebounds. That sent Washington to the WNBA Finals for the first time in team history.

2018 WNBA FINALS
Seattle Storms to the Title!

GAME 1 Seattle 89
Washington 76

Seattle usually depended on 2018 MVP **Breanna Stewart**. In Game 1, though, they were led by guard **Jewell Loyd**. She had a game-high 23 points and scored 10 consecutive points during a 16–4 run in the second quarter. That helped Seattle to a 16-point halftime lead that they never gave up. Stewart did her part with 20 points after struggling early in the game. Washington star **Elena Delle Donne** was not herself, as she battled a knee injury.

Stewart dominated the Finals and brought home MVP hardware.

GAME 2 Seattle 75
Washington 73

Stewart pushed back to the top of the scoring list in Game 2. She was clutch late in the game as Washington made a strong comeback run. Stewart scored six of Seattle's final seven points. A last-ditch effort by the Mystics fell short. Seattle took a 2–0 lead in the best-of-five series. They also continued a streak of never losing a WNBA Finals game at home.

GAME 3 Seattle 98
Washington 82

Stewart once again led the way, this time scoring 30 points as the Storm won the team's third WNBA championship. She was named the Finals MVP, averaging 25.6 points per game in the Storm's sweep. She got help in the final game from **Natasha Howard**, who scored 29. The win also gave veteran Seattle guard **Sue Bird** her third championship.

Super Season

The biggest news in the early season came from a pair of teams in the north. Toronto burst out of the starting gate, winning 20 of its first 25 games. To the south of that Canadian city, the Milwaukee Bucks were also surging, led by the incredible **Giannis Antetokounmpo**. They were especially hot in the middle of the season, losing only four games combined in January and February, while winning 22.

Philadelphia was another big story in the Eastern Conference. The team was in the second season of a huge comeback. The 76ers had spent several seasons before that losing a LOT of games. That earned them draft picks that packed their lineup with stars. **Joel Embiid** and **Ben Simmons** were joined by veteran guard **Jimmy Butler** to finally become the team they wanted.

NBA MVP
Giannis
Antetokounmpo

They ended with the conference's third-best record.

In the West, just about everyone seemed to have a chance in the first half of the season. Several teams traded places in the top spot. At one point, eight teams were within two games of first place. Five more were within four games. Only Phoenix was out of the party early.

The Denver Nuggets quickly proved to be a big challenge for the defending-champion Golden State Warriors. Serbian star **Nikola Jokic** moved into the ranks of the NBA's best. The Portland Trail Blazers boasted a top guard pair of **Damian Lillard** and **CJ McCollum**. The Houston Rockets, of course, were once again led by all-world **James Harden**, who put on a show for the ages. From December 13 to February 25, he scored at least 30 points in 32 games in a row. That was the second-longest such streak in NBA history. In that run, he had eighteen 40-point games and even four 50-point games!

Even though their team added the incredible **LeBron "The King" James**, Lakers fans didn't have much to cheer

Jokic helped the Nuggets soar in 2019.

about. LA missed the playoffs for the sixth straight season. James did get one thrill by returning to Cleveland and beating his old team, the Cavaliers.

By the time the regular season ended, Golden State was back on top in the West. A big reason was the great play of **Kevin Durant**. He led the team by averaging 26 points per game. In a November win over Toronto, he poured in a season-high 51.

Would the Warriors repeat? Or would a new team grab the crown? What would Canada say about the outcome? The playoffs offered a lot of chances for new teams to make a grab at the trophy. Keep reading to find out more about who came home a winner!

2018-19 Final Standings

EASTERN CONFERENCE

1.	Milwaukee	60–22
2.	Toronto	58–24
3.	Philadelphia	51–31
4.	Boston	49–33
5.	Indiana	48–34
6.	Brooklyn	42–40
7.	Orlando	42–40
8.	Detroit	41–41
9.	Charlotte	39–43
10.	Miami	39–43
11.	Washington	32–50
12.	Atlanta	29–53
13.	Chicago	22–60
14.	Cleveland	19–63
15.	New York	17–65

WESTERN CONFERENCE

1.	Golden State	57–25
2.	Denver	54–28
3.	Portland	53–29
4.	Houston	53–29
5.	Utah	50–32
6.	Oklahoma City	49–33
7.	San Antonio	48–34
8.	Clippers	48–34
9.	Sacramento	39–43
10.	Lakers	37–45
11.	Minnesota	36–46
12.	Memphis	33–49
13.	New Orleans	33–49
14.	Dallas	33–49
15.	Phoenix	19–63

In the Paint

One Wild Game!

The San Antonio Spurs and Oklahoma City Thunder nearly broke the scoreboard in the January 10 double-overtime game. San Antonio hung on to win 154–147, but along the way, the two teams put up some wild numbers. The last game to reach this points total came back in 2006! Spurs coach **Gregg Popovich** won his 1,222nd game. That pushed him to No. 3 all-time among coaches. The Spurs made 16 of 19 three-point shots for an 84.2 percentage; that's the best ever for a team that tried at least 15 threes. **LaMarcus Aldridge** led the way for the Spurs with a career-high 56 points . . . including zero three-pointers! Oklahoma City was behind by 16 in the fourth quarter . . . and came back to tie the game! **Russell Westbrook** was the first player ever with this stat line: 24 points, 24 assists, and 13 rebounds. The Spurs came home with the W, though.

Who Needs to Dribble?

Golden State's **Klay Thompson** is a great "catch-and-shoot" player, but what he did in January against the Knicks was crazy. He

Mr. Everything: Oklahoma City star Russell Westbrook continued to triple double!

scored 43 points, including hitting 7 three-pointers . . . and he only dribbled four times! That meant for nearly every basket, he took a pass from a teammate and shot the ball right away. When it's working, keep doing it!

New Three-Point Records ▶▶▶

Three-point baskets pour in night after night in the NBA. Nothing has made such a big change in the game. Where there are shots, of course, there are records. Helped by **James Harden** with six, the Houston Rockets poured in 26 "treys" in a December win over the Washington Wizards. That was a new NBA single-game record. In April, they matched that total in a victory against the Sacramento Kings. In January, the Golden State Warriors and Kings combined to make 41 in the game, the most ever by both teams in a game. Golden State's **Stephen Curry** had 10, including the record-breaker. The Warriors won 127–123.

LeBron Is No. 4!

To his fans, **LeBron James** is No. 1, of course, but we're talking about the NBA's career scoring list. With a layup against the Denver Nuggets, James moved past Michael Jordan into fourth place on the points list. Only **Kareem Abdul-Jabbar**, **Karl Malone**, and **Kobe Bryant** scored more points than "The King." He ended the 2018–19 season with 32,543 for his career.

Thanks, Kid!

Rajon Rondo spent most of nine seasons as a star with the Boston Celtics. In February 2019, he came back as a member of the Lakers. Before the game, he was getting some help warming up from his son, Pierre. "Guarded" by the seven-year-old, Rondo made a jumper from about 20 feet. Later, with the game on the line, that practice paid off. He buried a buzzer-beater from almost exactly the same spot to clinch a big Lakers win!

Mr. 20-20-20

Russell Westbrook is already Mr. Triple Double. This season, he averaged double digits in points, assists, and rebounds for the whole season . . . for the *third* year in a row! In an April win over the Lakers, the Thunder's all-around star put in 20 points, grabbed 20 boards, and dished 21 dimes. It was only the second time in NBA history that a player had reached 20 in all three categories in one game. (The first was Wilt Chamberlain in 1968.) Westbrook said after the game that his performance was to honor a friend, entertainer Nipsey Hussle, who had recently died. "Grateful to play the game, but that wasn't for me, man. That was for my bro, man. That was for Nipsey."

2019 NBA Playoffs

Here are some highlights of the wild April and May that led to the NBA Finals.

Record Battle: To start 2019's postseason, the LA Clippers faced the defending-champion Warriors. The Clips surprised many by taking two games from Golden State. In Game 2, they rallied from 31 points behind to set a new NBA playoff comeback record. It took a 50-point performance from **Kevin Durant** to finally put the Clips away in Game 6.

Nearly the Longest: Portland and Denver needed four overtimes to decide Game 3 of their second-round matchup. The Trail Blazers squeaked out with a 140–137 win. It was one overtime short of being the longest playoff game in NBA history, and was the longest since 1953.

Big Bad Bucks: Milwaukee continued its very successful season by mowing down the Pistons in four straight games and then beating Boston in five. They lost Game 1 to the Celtics, but that just got **Giannis Antetokounmpo** mad. He helped the Bucks win four games in a row again, including a 25-point win in the Game 5 clincher.

Buzzer Beater: The 76ers have been building their young team for a season like this. The team had the East's third-best record two seasons after losing 54 games! In the Eastern semis, Philly gave Toronto all it could handle. It came down to Game 7, when **Kawhi Leonard** buried an epic, buzzer-beating, game-winning, series-deciding three-pointer.

Yup, this Leonard game-winner went in!

2019 NBA FINALS
Raptors Romp!

Perhaps the most important thing in the 2019 NBA Finals was **Kevin Durant**'s leg. As Golden State beat the Houston Rockets in the conference semifinal, Durant injured his calf. He missed the final Rockets game and the whole conference final series victory over Portland. Could the Warriors beat the Raptors in the Finals without him?

Game 1 showed how much he was missed. **Stephen Curry** tried to make up for the loss with 34 points, but the Raptors depth was the difference. Three Toronto players topped 20 points, led by **Pascal Siakam**'s 32. In Game 2, the Warriors shut down every Raptor except **Kawhi Leonard**, who had 34 points. That was not enough, however, and Golden State evened the series.

In Game 3, the Warriors were also without **Klay Thompson**. Toronto took advantage. Leonard had 30 and **Kyle Lowry** added 23 more. That was more than enough to overcome Curry's 47 points.

Leonard poured it on in Game 4, scoring a career

Canada's new hero, Kawhi Leonard

Finals-high 36 points. Thompson was back to complete the "Splash Brothers," but the loss of Durant was still hurting the Dubs.

Game 5 added new drama to an exciting series. Durant was cleared to return for the must-win game. Trailing three games to one, the Warriors needed his help. Unfortunately, after scoring 11 points, he hurt his leg again and was out for good. His teammates had his back, though, and Thompson nailed a late three-pointer to clinch a one-point win.

Game 6 was the last one played at the Warriors' home at Oracle Arena. Toronto spoiled the party. Finals MVP Leonard poured in 22 points, while guard **Fred VanVleet** was a surprise star, with 22 points, including 12 in the final quarter. Canada celebrated its first NBA champions after the 114–110 win. Leonard became the first player to win a Finals NBA award for each conference (he also won with San Antonio in 2014). O Canada indeed!

NBA Awards

MOST VALUABLE PLAYER

GIANNIS ANTETOKOUNMPO

BUCKS

DEFENSIVE PLAYER OF THE YEAR

RUDY GOBERT

JAZZ

ROOKIE OF THE YEAR

LUKA DONČIĆ

MAVERICKS

SIXTH MAN

LOU WILLIAMS

CLIPPERS

MOST IMPROVED PLAYER

◄◄◄PASCAL SIAKAM

RAPTORS

COACH OF THE YEAR

MIKE BUDENHOLZER

BUCKS

COMMUNITY CARES AWARD

BRADLEY BEAL

WIZARDS

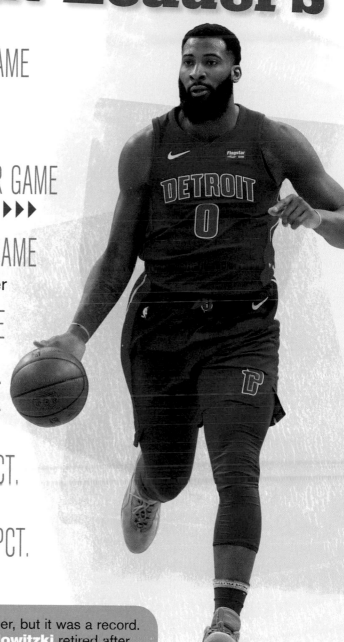

NBA Stat Leaders

36.1 POINTS PER GAME
378 3-POINTERS

James Harden, Rockets

15.6 REBOUNDS PER GAME

Andre Drummond, Pistons ▶▶▶

10.7 ASSISTS PER GAME

Russell Westbrook, Thunder

2.7 BLOCKS PER GAME

Myles Turner, Pacers

2.2 STEALS PER GAME

Paul George, Thunder

66.8 FIELD GOAL PCT.

Rudy Gobert, Jazz

92.8 FREE-THROW PCT.

Malcolm Brogdon, Bucks

21 It's not a big number, but it was a record. Dallas star **Dirk Nowitzki** retired after playing that many seasons. That's the most ever for a player with one team.

Stat Stuff

NBA CHAMPIONS

2018-19 **Toronto**	2003-04 **Detroit**	1988-89 **Detroit**
2017-18 **Golden State**	2002-03 **San Antonio**	1987-88 **LA Lakers**
2016-17 **Golden State**	2001-02 **LA Lakers**	1986-87 **LA Lakers**
2015-16 **Cleveland**	2000-01 **LA Lakers**	1985-86 **Boston**
2014-15 **Golden State**	1999-00 **LA Lakers**	1984-85 **LA Lakers**
2013-14 **San Antonio**	1998-99 **San Antonio**	1983-84 **Boston**
2012-13 **Miami**	1997-98 **Chicago**	1982-83 **Philadelphia**
2011-12 **Miami**	1996-97 **Chicago**	1981-82 **LA Lakers**
2010-11 **Dallas**	1995-96 **Chicago**	1980-81 **Boston**
2009-10 **LA Lakers**	1994-95 **Houston**	1979-80 **LA Lakers**
2008-09 **LA Lakers**	1993-94 **Houston**	1978-79 **Seattle**
2007-08 **Boston**	1992-93 **Chicago**	1977-78 **Washington**
2006-07 **San Antonio**	1991-92 **Chicago**	1976-77 **Portland**
2005-06 **Miami**	1990-91 **Chicago**	1975-76 **Boston**
2004-05 **San Antonio**	1989-90 **Detroit**	1974-75 **Golden State**

1973–74 **Boston**	1955–56 **Philadelphia**	1950–51 **Rochester**
1972–73 **New York**	1954–55 **Syracuse**	1949–50 **Minneapolis**
1971–72 **LA Lakers**	1953–54 **Minneapolis**	1948–49 **Minneapolis**
1970–71 **Milwaukee**	1952–53 **Minneapolis**	1947–48 **Baltimore**
1969–70 **New York**	1951–52 **Minneapolis**	1946–47 **Philadelphia**
1968–69 **Boston**		
1967–68 **Boston**		

WNBA CHAMPIONS

1966–67 **Philadelphia**	2018 **Seattle**	2007 **Phoenix**
1965–66 **Boston**	2017 **Minnesota**	2006 **Detroit**
1964–65 **Boston**	2016 **Los Angeles**	2005 **Sacramento**
1963–64 **Boston**	2015 **Minnesota**	2004 **Seattle**
1962–63 **Boston**	2014 **Phoenix**	2003 **Detroit**
1961–62 **Boston**	2013 **Minnesota**	2002 **Los Angeles**
1960–61 **Boston**	2012 **Indiana**	2001 **Los Angeles**
1959–60 **Boston**	2011 **Minnesota**	2000 **Houston**
1958–59 **Boston**	2010 **Seattle**	1999 **Houston**
1957–58 **St. Louis**	2009 **Phoenix**	1998 **Houston**
1956–57 **Boston**	2008 **Detroit**	1997 **Houston**

NHL

THESE GUYS DO *NOT HAVE THE BLUES!*
A pile of happy St. Louis Blues celebrate winning the first Stanley Cup in team history. Their victory in Game 7 over the Boston Bruins capped off an amazing turnaround. In January, the Blues were the worst team in the league. By June, they were the best! Read more about their story and other highlights from another exciting NHL season.

Tampa Bay's Nikita Kucherov's 128 points were the most ever by an NHL player from Russia.

A Season of Comebacks

On January 3, 2019, the Tampa Bay Lightning had 32 wins and just nine losses, and were well on their way to setting an NHL record for wins. They almost did, ending the season with 62 wins and tying the record set by the 1995–96 Detroit Red Wings (a team with seven future Hall of Famers). The Lightning scored 319 goals and had a power play that scored more than 28 percent of the time—compared to a league average of just over 18 percent.

On January 3, the St. Louis Blues had 16 wins and 22 losses. They were last in the NHL. They had fired their head coach in November, and named assistant **Craig Berube** temporary head coach. In early December, Berube brought up goaltender **Jordan Binnington** from the minor leagues. The Blues ended up going on a 30-10-5 run, and squeaked into the playoffs.

So it was a pretty big surprise in hockey land when, on June 12, the Blues raised the Stanley Cup and the Lightning watched from home! The record-matching team had been knocked out in a startling first-round sweep by Columbus weeks before. It was the end of an NHL season that was marked by more goal-scoring than the league had ever seen: 7,664 goals, to be exact. That's an average of six per game—although it does include 87 goals in shootouts.

The goal-scoring came from everywhere. Six players had 100 points or more this season, which hasn't happened in more than a decade. They were **Nikita Kucherov** of the Lightning (128 points); **Connor McDavid** of the Edmonton Oilers (116); **Patrick Kane** of the Chicago Blackhawks (110); **Leon Draisaitl** of the Edmonton Oilers (105); **Brad Marchand** of the Boston Bruins (100); and **Sidney Crosby** of the Pittsburgh Penguins. It was Crosby's

FINAL STANDINGS

EASTERN CONFERENCE		WESTERN CONFERENCE	
PLACE/TEAM	POINTS	PLACE/TEAM	POINTS
1. LIGHTNING	128	1. FLAMES	107
2. BRUINS	107	2. SHARKS	101
3. CAPITALS	104	3. PREDATORS	100
4. ISLANDERS	103	4. JETS	99
5. MAPLE LEAFS	100	5. BLUES	99
6. PENGUINS	100	6. STARS	93
7. HURRICANES	99	7. GOLDEN KNIGHTS	93
8. BLUE JACKETS	98	8. AVALANCHE	90
9. CANADIENS	96	9. COYOTES	86
10. PANTHERS	86	10. BLACKHAWKS	84
11. FLYERS	82	11. WILD	83
12. RANGERS	78	12. CANUCKS	81
13. SABRES	76	13. DUCKS	80
14. RED WINGS	74	14. OILERS	79
15. DEVILS	72	15. KINGS	71
16. SENATORS	64		

Crosby reached a century again!

sixth "century" season (100 years = a century, get it?).

For the eighth time in his career, **Alexander Ovechkin** of the Washington Capitals scored 50 goals or more. At age 33, Ovechkin has led the NHL in goals more times (also eight) than any other player in league history. He was joined in the 50-goal club by **Leon Draisaitl** of the Edmonton Oilers, who had a career-best season with 50 of his own.

All those goals meant plenty of clawbacks and comebacks during the regular season. Teams came back to win after being two or more goals down in 138 games, another NHL record. And overall, the teams that were trailing by at least one goal ended up winning 41 percent of the time. All those stats meant that no lead was safe in the NHL in 2019.

Hockey Highlights

GLOBE-HOPPING Because everyone, everywhere loves hockey (right?), the NHL played two preseason games in China and two in Europe. The Calgary Flames and Boston Bruins faced off in Shenzhen and again in Beijing. In Europe, the New Jersey Devils took on the home team in Bern, Switzerland, and the Edmonton Oilers faced the local team in Cologne, Germany. Three regular-season games moved to Scandinavia. The Edmonton Oilers and New Jersey Devils played in Gothenburg, Sweden, in October, and the Florida Panthers and Winnipeg Jets played two games in Helsinki, Finland, in November.

ISLANDER-HOPPING

Unhappy with their home at the Barclays Center in Brooklyn, the New York Islanders moved half of their home games to their old arena at the Veterans Memorial Coliseum. In the playoffs, the first round was in Nassau and the second round in Brooklyn. The 2019–20 season will be the same, with home games split between the two arenas. Plans haven't yet been announced for the 2020–21 season, but the final goal, slated for 2021–22, is a new stadium, the Belmont Park Arena, located right next to the famous Belmont Park horseracing track.

GROWING AGAIN

On December 4, Commissioner **Gary Bettman** announced that the league will add a new team in Seattle that will begin play in the 2021–22 season, at a new arena that is being built just for them. The still-unnamed Seattle team will be in the Pacific Division, and the Arizona Coyotes will move to the Central Division.

2019 NHL ENTRY DRAFT

Some of the finest young hockey players in the world were available in the 2019 NHL Entry Draft. American center **Jack Hughes** and Finnish forward **Kaapo Kakko** were the favorites. Hughes, a speedy, skilled

Jack Hughes

player, went with the first overall pick to the Devils. Kakko, an electrifying offensive threat, is heading to the Rangers after being picked second. With the two teams facing off across the Hudson River, it will be exciting to see these young players create a local rivalry.

21ST-CENTURY MAN

On October 3, Montreal Canadiens forward **Jesperi Kotkaniemi** became the first person born in the 21st century to be a pro athlete in any of the four major North American men's leagues (NHL, NFL, NBA, and MLB).

GOT GOALIES?

On March 1, the Philadelphia Flyers set an NHL record by using eight goaltenders in one season. (For the record and in case they're reading this, they were **Brian Elliott**, **Calvin Pickard**, **Michal Neuvirth**, **Alex Lyon**, **Anthony Stolarz**, **Carter Hart**, **Mike McKenna**, and **Cam Talbot**.) Repeated injuries to the men in net were the reason.

LUONGO LEAVES AND OPRIK EXITS

Goalie **Roberto Luongo**, who spent time with the Islanders, Canucks, and Panthers, retired after 19 seasons, 1,044 games, a .919 career save percentage, five NHL All-Star appearances, and two Olympic gold medals. Luongo's 489 wins are third in NHL history. After a 16-season NHL career, defenseman **Brooks Orpik** announced his retirement. He won two Stanley Cups—with the Pittsburgh Penguins in 2009 and the Washington Capitals in 2018. He said his initial goal was to play in just one NHL game, but he ended up playing in 1,035 of them!

ROOKIE SENSATION

One of the most surprising and important players to help the St. Louis Blues win their first Stanley Cup was 25-year-old goaltender **Jordan Binnington**. He began the season playing for the minor-league San Antonio Rampage, and he had never played an NHL game until the Blues called him to join the club in December. He led the Blues to an incredible run of victories, winning nine straight games from January to February, the longest win streak for a Blues rookie goaltender. He won a total of 24 games, with five shutouts (a team rookie record) and was the first rookie goaltender to finish a season with a goals-against average of 1.89 or lower. He was also one of five goalies in NHL history to record 20 wins in his first 25 or fewer starts.

2019 Playoffs

The Blue Jackets (right) turned off the Lightning.

The 2019 Stanley Cup playoffs will be remembered for shocking upsets: For the first time in league history, all the division winners were knocked out in the first round.

The Tampa Bay Lightning were heavily favored against their first-round opponent, the Columbus Blue Jackets. Tampa took a 3–0 lead in Game 1, but Columbus roared back to win. Tampa never recovered and were swept in four games. The 2018 Stanley Cup-champion Washington Capitals also made a first-round exit. So did the Pittsburgh Penguins, who were swept by the New York Islanders—who were then brushed away in four games in the next round by the Carolina Hurricanes. Amazingly, the broom came out again when the Boston Bruins knocked out the Hurricanes in four games. It was sweep, sweep, sweep!

There were additional surprises. The Dallas Stars pushed out the always-dangerous Nashville Predators, while the San Jose Sharks won a dramatic seven-game series against last year's Cup finalist Vegas Golden Knights in round one. The Calgary Flames had a tremendous season and finished at the top of their division, but they were eliminated in five games by the Colorado Avalanche. The Boston Bruins went back and forth with a talented Toronto Maple Leafs team before finishing them off in a tense seven games to make the Cup final.

The St. Louis Blues had a dramatic road to the Cup, too. After knocking out the favored Winnipeg Jets in round one, they battled the Dallas Stars in a thrilling seven-game series that ended with Blues veteran forward **Paul Maroon** poking home a rebound for the series-winning goal in the second nail-biting overtime period. After sending the San Jose Sharks home in the conference final, they were ready to face off against the Bruins for the Stanley Cup.

2019 Stanley Cup Final

The Blues had never won a Stanley Cup. The last time they even came close was way back in 1970. Their opponent then and in 2019 was the Boston Bruins. The Blues were hoping history would not be repeated.

St. Louis jumped out to a 2–0 lead in Game 1, but Boston bounced back to win. Game 2 was a thriller. The teams combined for four first-period goals. Late in the game Blues defenseman **Carl Gunnarson** fired a shot that rang off the goalpost but did not go in. Before heading onto the ice for overtime, Gunnarson told coach **Craig Berube**, "I need one more." He got it. Early in the overtime, Gunnarson's wrist shot found the back of the net to win the game.

When the series moved to St. Louis, the Bruins quieted the cheering hometown fans with a crushing 7–2 victory. Two nights later, the Blues tied the series again.

In Game 5, rookie goaltender **Jordan Binnington** stopped 38 Bruins shots; St. Louis won 2–1. In Game 6, the Bruins spoiled a St. Louis celebration with a 5–1 win that sent the series to Game 7.

In Boston, the Bruins came out storming the net. But it was Blues center **Ryan O'Reilly** who struck first, deflecting in a shot. Then Blues captain **Alex Pietrangelo** lifted a backhand shot with only eight seconds left in the first period, and the Bruins fans were silenced. When the final buzzer sounded, the score was 4–1 and the Blues celebrated their first Stanley Cup victory.

Can you find the puck? Let's just say if you do, it will make the Blues very happy!

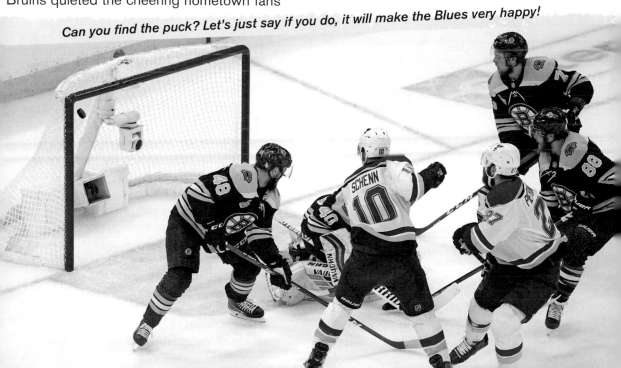

2018–19 Awards

Pettersson was the top rookie.

Hart Trophy
(Most Valuable Player)

Ted Lindsay Award
(MVP as voted by players)

Art Ross Trophy
(Highest scorer)
NIKITA KUCHEROV, Lightning

Vezina Trophy
(Top Goaltender)
ANDREI VASILEVSKIY, Lightning

Calder Trophy
(Best Rookie)
ELIAS PETTERSSON, Canucks

Norris Trophy
(Best Defenseman)
MARK GIORDANO, Flames

Selke Trophy
(Best Defensive Forward)
RYAN O'REILLY, Blues

Maurice Richard Trophy
(Top Goal Scorer)
ALEXANDER OVECHKIN, Capitals

Lady Byng Trophy
(Sportsmanship)
ALEKSANDER BARKOV, Panthers

Masterton Trophy
(Dedication to Hockey)
ROBIN LEHNER, Islanders

Mark Messier Leadership Award
WAYNE SIMMONDS, Predators

Jack Adams Award
(Coach of the Year)
BARRY TROTZ, Islanders

NHL Stat Champs

128 POINTS
87 ASSISTS
Nikita Kucherov, Lightning

51 GOALS ▶▶▶
Alexander Ovechkin, Capitals

+39 PLUS-MINUS
Mark Giordano, Flames

1.89 GOALS AGAINST AVG.
Jordan Binnington, Blues

.934 SAVE PERCENTAGE
Ben Bishop, Stars

39 GOALIE WINS
Andrei Vasilevskiy, Lightning

❝I have to be healthy, I have to be in good shape. I'm going to try to do it, but you don't know what's going to happen in the future.❞

— **ALEXANDER OVECHKIN** WHEN ASKED IF HE CAN CHALLENGE WAYNE GRETZKY'S RECORD OF 894 GOALS

Stanley Cup Champions

2018–19	**St. Louis Blues**		1991–92	**Pittsburgh Penguins**
2017–18	**Washington Capitals**		1990–91	**Pittsburgh Penguins**
2016–17	**Pittsburgh Penguins**		1989–90	**Edmonton Oilers**
2015–16	**Pittsburgh Penguins**		1988–89	**Calgary Flames**
2014–15	**Chicago Blackhawks**		1987–88	**Edmonton Oilers**
2013–14	**Los Angeles Kings**		1986–87	**Edmonton Oilers**
2012–13	**Chicago Blackhawks**		1985–86	**Montreal Canadiens**
2011–12	**Los Angeles Kings**		1984–85	**Edmonton Oilers**
2010–11	**Boston Bruins**		1983–84	**Edmonton Oilers**
2009–10	**Chicago Blackhawks**		1982–83	**New York Islanders**
2008–09	**Pittsburgh Penguins**		1981–82	**New York Islanders**
2007–08	**Detroit Red Wings**		1980–81	**New York Islanders**
2006–07	**Anaheim Ducks**		1979–80	**New York Islanders**
2005–06	**Carolina Hurricanes**		1978–79	**Montreal Canadiens**
2004–05	No champion (Lockout)		1977–78	**Montreal Canadiens**
2003–04	**Tampa Bay Lightning**		1976–77	**Montreal Canadiens**
2002–03	**New Jersey Devils**		1975–76	**Montreal Canadiens**
2001–02	**Detroit Red Wings**		1974–75	**Philadelphia Flyers**
2000–01	**Colorado Avalanche**		1973–74	**Philadelphia Flyers**
1999–00	**New Jersey Devils**		1972–73	**Montreal Canadiens**
1998–99	**Dallas Stars**		1971–72	**Boston Bruins**
1997–98	**Detroit Red Wings**		1970–71	**Montreal Canadiens**
1996–97	**Detroit Red Wings**		1969–70	**Boston Bruins**
1995–96	**Colorado Avalanche**		1968–69	**Montreal Canadiens**
1994–95	**New Jersey Devils**		1967–68	**Montreal Canadiens**
1993–94	**New York Rangers**		1966–67	**Toronto Maple Leafs**
1992–93	**Montreal Canadiens**		1965–66	**Montreal Canadiens**

1964–65	**Montreal Canadiens**
1963–64	**Toronto Maple Leafs**
1962–63	**Toronto Maple Leafs**
1961–62	**Toronto Maple Leafs**
1960–61	**Chicago Blackhawks**
1959–60	**Montreal Canadiens**
1958–59	**Montreal Canadiens**
1957–58	**Montreal Canadiens**
1956–57	**Montreal Canadiens**
1955–56	**Montreal Canadiens**

MOST STANLEY CUP TITLES

Montreal Canadiens	**23**
Toronto Maple Leafs	**13**
Detroit Red Wings	**11**
Boston Bruins	**6**
Chicago Blackhawks	**6**

1954–55	**Detroit Red Wings**		1935–36	**Detroit Red Wings**
1953–54	**Detroit Red Wings**		1934–35	**Montreal Maroons**
1952–53	**Montreal Canadiens**		1933–34	**Chicago Blackhawks**
1951–52	**Detroit Red Wings**		1932–33	**New York Rangers**
1950–51	**Toronto Maple Leafs**		1931–32	**Toronto Maple Leafs**
1949–50	**Detroit Red Wings**		1930–31	**Montreal Canadiens**
1948–49	**Toronto Maple Leafs**		1929–30	**Montreal Canadiens**
1947–48	**Toronto Maple Leafs**		1928–29	**Boston Bruins**
1946–47	**Toronto Maple Leafs**		1927–28	**New York Rangers**
1945–46	**Montreal Canadiens**		1926–27	**Ottawa Senators**
1944–45	**Toronto Maple Leafs**		1925–26	**Montreal Maroons**
1943–44	**Montreal Canadiens**		1924–25	**Montreal Canadiens**
1942–43	**Detroit Red Wings**		1923–24	**Montreal Canadiens**
1941–42	**Toronto Maple Leafs**		1922–23	**Ottawa Senators**
1940–41	**Boston Bruins**		1921–22	**Toronto St. Patricks**
1939–40	**New York Rangers**		1920–21	**Ottawa Senators**
1938–39	**Boston Bruins**		1919–20	**Ottawa Senators**
1937–38	**Chicago Blackhawks**		1918–19	**Montreal Canadiens**
1936–37	**Detroit Red Wings**		1917–18	**Toronto Arenas**

62
2
DISCOUNT TIRE
WÜRTH
SKF
NASCAR HEAT
AXALTA
MONSTER
24
40
SIEMENS

SEAT BELTS, EVERYONE!
This was the wild scene toward the end of the 2019 Daytona 500. After this and another wreck, more than 24 cars had been knocked out of NASCAR's biggest race. Check out the final race results on page 129. And follow along the tire tracks of the whole 2018 NASCAR season inside!

NASCAR

A lucky fan in Texas got a picture with race winner Kevin Harvick.

Another Wild Ride!

Hot starts don't always end up with top finishes. The 2018 NASCAR champion hung back during the summer before roaring to the top. How did he get there?

Three drivers dominated the first half of the season. Defending champion Martin Truex, Jr. got off to a slow start, but won at Fontana in the sixth race of the year. He took the checkered flag twice more by mid-July. Two other drivers roared ahead of him, however. Kevin Harvick won three races in a row in March for a flying start. He added back-to-back wins in May at Dover and Kansas. Kyle Busch matched Harvick's threepeat in April and won two more races before midseason as well. Not surprisingly, all three were well ahead of the rest of the field.

Joining them among the race winners was Joey Logano. The 28-year-old was the only one of the four without a NASCAR season championship. He came on strong late in the season, though. After earning his spot in the playoffs with a win at Talladega, he piled up points in late-season races.

When the Chase began, Logano was at his best. He had five top-five races in the 10 playoff races. With a final-race victory in Miami, Logano joined those other great drivers with big trophies. He emerged from the Chase for the Cup as the 2018 champion.

Along the way to Logano's big title, NASCAR provided many other great stories for fans.

An early season surprise was Austin Dillon winning the Daytona 500 in the famous No. 3 car of the late Dale Earnhardt, Sr. It was Dillon's second career victory. Later in the summer, Erik

CHASE FOR THE CUP!
2018 FINAL STANDINGS

PLACE/RACER	POINTS
1. **Joey Logano**	5,040
2. **Martin Truex, Jr.**	5,035
3. **Kevin Harvick**	5,034
4. **Kyle Busch**	5,033
5. **Aric Almirola**	2,354
6. **Chase Elliott**	2,350
7. **Kurt Busch**	2,350
8. **Brad Keselowski**	2,343
9. **Kyle Larson**	2,299
10. **Ryan Blaney**	2,298
11. **Denny Hamlin**	2,285
12. **Clint Bowyer**	2,272

Jones earned his first Cup victory, winning a race at Daytona in July. Chase Elliott won at Watkins Glen for his first NASCAR checkered flag. Greeting him at the finish was his dad, "Million Dollar" Bill Elliott, a NASCAR Hall of Famer!

Fans of fender-bending racing got plenty to cheer. Kyle Busch bumped Kyle Larson out of the way to win at Chicago. In a key playoff race, Jimmie Johnson and Truex clanged together on the next-to-last turn of the Charlotte "Roval" race, and Ryan Blaney snuck between their spinning cars for a dramatic win. The Roval itself was big news, as the famed Charlotte track was morphed into a combination of oval and street course, with multiple twists and turns.

The 2018 Chase for the Cup had plenty of twists and turns, too. Read on to find out how the playoffs unfolded on the track!

One for Dad! Chase Elliott brought home his first NASCAR win at Watkins Glen.

2018: CHASE FOR THE CUP!

Ryan Blaney (12) won at Charlotte when Jimmie Johnson (48) and Martin Truex, Jr. (78) crashed.

ROUND 1

LAS VEGAS: Brad Keselowski kept his late-season hot streak going as the playoff chase began. He won his third race in a row, but he needed overtime laps to get it done. In the final restart, he held off Kyle Larson.

RICHMOND: Kyle Busch added another checkered flag to his great 2018 season. He clinched a spot in the next round with a big win in Richmond. It was his seventh race win of the year, tied with Kevin Harvick for the most so far.

CHARLOTTE: In a race held on a twisting track with 17 turns, Ryan Blaney held on for a big win and a spot in the next round. Blaney avoided a last-pass crash and won by less than a second over Jamie McMurray.

OUT: Austin Dillon, Denny Hamlin, Jimmie Johnson, Erik Jones

ROUND 2

DOVER: A crash with four laps left knocked out several top drivers and set up a dramatic overtime finish. Chase Elliott roared out on the restart and held on for a big win that put him in the next round of the playoffs.

TALLADEGA: Aric Almirola was in the right place at the right time. He trailed Kurt Busch on the final lap when Busch ran out of gas! Almirola swept by to win the race and earn a spot in the next round of the Chase.

KANSAS: Elliott won again, holding off Larson on the last lap. Joey Logano had a great race, winning Stage 1. That helped him get enough points to move on to the next round. Big things were coming for him, however.

OUT: Ryan Blaney, Alex Bowman, Brad Keselowski, Kyle Larson

ROUND 3

MARTINSVILLE: Logano became the first driver to clinch a spot in the final four by winning in West Virginia. He had to play bumper cars to come out on top. On the last lap, he shoved the rear of **Martin Truex, Jr.**, spinning Truex enough for Logano to race by for the victory. No, Truex was not pleased!

TEXAS: Two down, two to go: **Kevin Harvick** won in overtime, seemingly to clinch the second spot in the Chase final. However, his team was penalized for an illegal car part. Harvick had 40 points taken from his total. His win here did not clinch his spot after all.

PHOENIX: **Kyle Busch** roared to victory here to earn the second spot in the Chase final. Harvick ended up with enough points to make it to Miami, even after the car-part disaster in Texas. Defending champion Truex rounded out the final four.

OUT: **Aric Almirola, Kurt Busch, Clint Bowyer, Chase Elliott**

CHAMPIONSHIP

MIAMI: Four drivers entered the season's final race at Homestead Raceway with a chance to win the 2018 NASCAR championship. Three of them were already season champs: Truex (2017), Kyle Busch (2015), and Harvick (2014). The fourth was Logano. The race saw several lead changes and each of the four had a shot at winning. With a powerful pass 12 laps from the end, Logano roared past Truex to join those other drivers in earning a season title. After winning the Miami race, he held up the season trophy with his 11-month-old son, Hudson.

Logano (22) waved the championship flag and took home this huge trophy!

Other NASCAR Champs

Brett Moffitt hung on for his first championship.

TRUCK RACING

Believe it or not, **Brett Moffitt** had never raced his truck on a 1.5-mile track before the 2018 Camping World Truck Series championship race at Miami. There, he was one of four drivers with a shot at the title. Moffitt made sure he got the season trophy by winning the race. After he took the lead late, he said, "The last 12 laps were the longest of my life!" It was the first NASCAR title for Moffitt.

XFINITY

Christopher Bell had a chance at a rare double. He was the 2017 Truck Series champ. In 2018, he had a shot at the Xfinity Series title. The XFinity Series is a steppingstone to NASCAR's top stock-car level. Bell made it exciting, winning the next-to-last race in Arizona to clinch his spot in the 200-lap championship race in Miami. However, he was passed on the outside during Lap 164 by **Tyler Reddick**. Reddick held on for another 36 dramatic laps to earn his first championship.

Tyler Reddick leads the way.

The official time difference between these two racers? 0.00 seconds!

Track Notes

Photo Finish

That's what racers call an event that is so close at the end that only a photo can show who won. In the Xfinity race in February 2018 at Daytona, it took a magnifying glass, too! Tyler Reddick beat Elliott Sadler by—officially—0.00 seconds. How is that possible? Reddick's car was ahead of Sadler's by so little that the clock couldn't measure the difference between the two! And yes, it was the closest race in NASCAR history!

Checkered Souvenir

A bunch of kids could be looking at a very cool souvenir hanging in their room right now. Ryan Blaney started a tradition at Dover in 2017 of giving away the checkered flag after his wins. And he kept it up in 2018! Then other drivers started copying him! Keelan Harvick got his dad's flag once, and other kids enjoyed getting flags and meeting their favorite drivers. Why does Blaney give away the flag? "Well, we get a trophy," he said.

2019 Daytona 500

Things were going along fine at the 2019 Daytona 500. Fans were enjoying tight racing, and the drivers were avoiding wrecks. Toward the end, though, things got a little crazy! About 10 laps from the end, a single wreck took out 18 cars! The race had to be stopped for more than a half hour to clean up. But wait, there was more. After the restart, another crash involved six cars. Out of all the broken metal, Denny Hamlin stayed undamaged. He roared to his second Daytona 500 win, holding off 2018 NASCAR champ Joey Logano.

NASCAR Champions

YEAR	DRIVER	CAR MAKER	YEAR	DRIVER	CAR MAKER
2018	Joey Logano	Ford	1996	Terry Labonte	Chevrolet
2017	Martin Truex, Jr.	Toyota	1995	Jeff Gordon	Chevrolet
2016	Jimmie Johnson	Chevrolet	1994	Dale Earnhardt, Sr.	Chevrolet
2015	Kyle Busch	Toyota	1993	Dale Earnhardt, Sr.	Chevrolet
2014	Kevin Harvick	Chevrolet	1992	Alan Kulwicki	Ford
2013	Jimmie Johnson	Chevrolet	1991	Dale Earnhardt, Sr.	Chevrolet
2012	Brad Keselowski	Dodge	1990	Dale Earnhardt, Sr.	Chevrolet
2011	Tony Stewart	Chevrolet	1989	Rusty Wallace	Pontiac
2010	Jimmie Johnson	Chevrolet	1988	Bill Elliott	Ford
2009	Jimmie Johnson	Chevrolet	1987	Dale Earnhardt, Sr.	Chevrolet
2008	Jimmie Johnson	Chevrolet	1986	Dale Earnhardt, Sr.	Chevrolet
2007	Jimmie Johnson	Chevrolet	1985	Darrell Waltrip	Chevrolet
2006	Jimmie Johnson	Chevrolet	1984	Terry Labonte	Chevrolet
2005	Tony Stewart	Chevrolet	1983	Bobby Allison	Buick
2004	Kurt Busch	Ford	1982	Darrell Waltrip	Buick
2003	Matt Kenseth	Ford	1981	Darrell Waltrip	Buick
2002	Tony Stewart	Pontiac	1980	Dale Earnhardt, Sr.	Chevrolet
2001	Jeff Gordon	Chevrolet	1979	Richard Petty	Chevrolet
2000	Bobby Labonte	Pontiac	1978	Cale Yarborough	Oldsmobile
1999	Dale Jarrett	Ford	1977	Cale Yarborough	Chevrolet
1998	Jeff Gordon	Chevrolet	1976	Cale Yarborough	Chevrolet
1997	Jeff Gordon	Chevrolet	1975	Richard Petty	Dodge

YEAR	DRIVER	CAR MAKER
1974	Richard Petty	Dodge
1973	Benny Parsons	Chevrolet
1972	Richard Petty	Plymouth
1971	Richard Petty	Plymouth
1970	Bobby Isaac	Dodge
1969	David Pearson	Ford
1968	David Pearson	Ford
1967	Richard Petty	Plymouth
1966	David Pearson	Dodge
1965	Ned Jarrett	Ford
1964	Richard Petty	Plymouth
1963	Joe Weatherly	Pontiac
1962	Joe Weatherly	Pontiac

YEAR	DRIVER	CAR MAKER
1961	Ned Jarrett	Chevrolet
1960	Rex White	Chevrolet
1959	Lee Petty	Plymouth
1958	Lee Petty	Oldsmobile
1957	Buck Baker	Chevrolet
1956	Buck Baker	Chrysler
1955	Tim Flock	Chrysler
1954	Lee Petty	Chrysler
1953	Herb Thomas	Hudson
1952	Tim Flock	Hudson
1951	Herb Thomas	Hudson
1950	Bill Rexford	Oldsmobile
1949	Red Byron	Oldsmobile

2020 NASCAR HALL OF FAME CLASS

Buddy Baker: This high-speed driver set the track record at Daytona in 1980 and won 19 NASCAR races.

Joe Gibbs: Gibbs is used to being in a Hall of Fame. After winning three Super Bowls as the coach of the Washington Redskins, he entered the Pro Football Hall of Fame in 1996. He is now in the NASCAR HOF for owning the racing team that has won four NASCAR championships.

Bobby Labonte: His 2000 NASCAR championship made it three for the Labonte family. Brother Terry won in 1984 and 1996.

Tony Stewart: One of the best-known drivers of recent years, Stewart was the champion in 2002, 2005, and 2011. He won 49 races and then became a team owner, winning the title with Kevin Harvick in 2015.

Waddell Wilson: Wilson built the engines of three series champions before becoming a top crew chief.

OTHER MOTOR SPORTS

MAKING A SPLASH!
Somewhere under all that splashing milk is the happy winner of the 2019 Indianpolis 500. Having milk for the winner in Victory Lane is a tradition dating back to the 1950s. The race itself dates back to 1911. So who is under that waterfall? *Turn to page 137 to find out!*

Great Britain's Lewis Hamilton joins the greats!

Formula 1: 2018

Lewis **Hamilton** must like visiting Mexico. For the second Formula 1 season in a row, the British driver clinched the season title in the Mexico City race. It was a historic win. Hamilton tied Argentina's **Juan Manuel Fangio** with five F1 titles. That's the second-most all-time behind Germany's **Michael Schumacher** (seven championships).

Getting his victory lap was a long, hard road for Hamilton. Early in the year, four-time champ **Sebastian Vettel** was off to a hot start. He won the first two races of the season to set the pace in driver points. Hamilton got points back

A crash in Germany doomed Vettel's hopes.

THE TOP THREE ALL-TIME
FORMULA 1 CHAMPIONSHIPS

7 **Michael Schumacher**, Germany
1994, 1995, 2000, 2001, 2002, 2003, 2004

5 **Lewis Hamilton**, Great Britain
2008, 2014, 2015, 2017, 2018

Juan Manuel Fangio, Argentina
1951, 1954, 1955, 1956, 1957

the top five of the final nine races of the year, including seven times in the top three. Watch for him near the front of races in 2019 and beyond. **Valtteri Bottas** suffered a tough loss at Baku. Leading and heading to victory, the Finnish driver suddenly got a flat tire three laps from the end. He couldn't even finish the race. A win would have put him atop the driver standings for the first time! But it was not to be.

Hamilton roared into 2019 hoping to break the tie with Fangio, but Vettel was going after his own fifth championship. Keep your eyes on the track to see who won!

with wins in Spain and Baku. Vettel won on Hamilton's home turf in the British Grand Prix and stayed just ahead of the defending champ.

Then Hamilton returned the favor. In the German Grand Prix, German star Vettel was on his way to victory and points that would extend his series lead. Then he crashed, and Hamilton won. The points swing pushed the British star into first place overall. He never gave up that spot.

On a roll, Hamilton won his fifth race in a row in Japan to get one step closer to yet another title. In that race, Vettel crashed again while trying to make a big move. He ended up far behind. The British ace led the series standings by 67 points going into the Texas F1 stop.

The race in Austin, Texas—the only US Formula 1 event—gave fans a thrill. The top three finishers were 2.3 seconds apart. **Kimi Räikkönen** won, just ahead of **Max Verstappen** and Hamilton.

Verstappen trailed from the start in the overall standings, but he moved up the rankings. The young Belgian who competes under the Dutch flag finished in

2018 FORMULA 1 TOP DRIVERS

PLACE/DRIVER/TEAM	POINTS
1. **Lewis HAMILTON**, Mercedes	408
2. **Sebastian VETTEL**, Ferrari	320
3. **Kimi RÄIKKÖNEN**, Ferrari	251
4. **Max VERSTAPPEN**, Red Bull	249
5. **Valtteri BOTTAS**, Mercedes	247
6. **Daniel RICCIARDO**, Red Bull	170
7. **Nico HÜLKENBERG**, Renault	69
8. **Sergio PÉREZ**, Force India	62
9. **Kevin MAGNUSSEN**, Haas	56
10. **Carlos SAINZ Jr.**, Renault	53

2018 IndyCar

Talk about good timing. In the final race of the 2018 IndyCar season, **Scott Dixon** ran out of gas just as he passed the finish line at Sonoma Raceway. He ended up second in the race, but that earned him enough points to clinch his fifth career IndyCar season title. He is the second driver ever with five; **A. J. Foyt** earned seven in his great career. (See box.)

Dixon finishing on top was nothing new for 2018, however. The New Zealander tied for the season lead with three race victories.

Dixon took the overall lead with his second race, which came in Fort Worth,

2018 INDYCAR FINAL STANDINGS

PLACE/DRIVER	POINTS
1. Scott DIXON	678
2. Alexander ROSSI	621
3. Will POWER	582
4. Ryan HUNTER-REAY	566
5. Josef NEWGARDEN	560

He knows what it's like to win—Scott Dixon roared to his fifth career IndyCar title.

2019 INDY 500
SO CLOSE!

The top Indy-car racers battled for 500 miles at the famous Indianapolis 500. After all that, **Simon Pagenaud** won by only two-tenths of a second over rival **Alexander Rossi**. The French driver started from the pole position and led for 116 laps, but Rossi was on his back wheels for most of them. The final laps were a back-and-forth duel as Pagenaud tried to hold off Rossi's many attempts to pass. After nipping Rossi at the checkered flag, Pagenaud enjoyed a bath in the traditional quart of milk given to Indy 500 winners. (See page 133!)

Texas. His third victory came in Toronto and cemented his spot atop the season standings. Winning is great, but finishing near the top is the way to pile up the points you need to take home the season trophy. In the 17 2018 races, Dixon was in the top three overall nine times! Dixon nearly doubled his lead over **Josef Newgarden** with the Toronto win and never really looked back.

For his part, Newgarden, the defending champ, finished a disappointing fifth overall after winning two of the season's first four races. **Alexander Rossi**, meanwhile, had his best overall finish ever. He was second behind Dixon, thanks in part to winning at Long Beach, Ohio, and Pocono.

The 2018 season also featured an action-packed Indy 500 that included 30 lead changes. Fifteen racers led the race at different points. Veteran star **Will Power** ended up leading at the checkered flag. Fans and fellow racers alike enjoyed watching his victory celebration. It was the Australian star's first win at the most famous race in the world.

IndyCar overall enjoyed a great 2018 season, with good TV ratings, great racing, and excited fans. New teams and drivers jumped into the 2019 season with hopes of continuing a solid run for the series.

THE TOP TWO ALL-TIME INDYCAR CHAMPIONSHIPS

7 **A. J. Foyt**, United States
1960, 1961, 1963, 1964, 1967, 1975, 1979

5 **Scott Dixon**, New Zealand
2003, 2008, 2013, 2015, 2018

Drag Racing Champs

Steve Torrence won his first Top Fuel title.

his dust and claim his first Top Fuel championship. It was the clincher on a great season for Torrence, who won 11 races overall. Believe it or not, one of the racers Torrence beat on his way to the title was his father, **Billy**!

FUNNY CAR

Former Top Fuel racer **J. R. Todd** is glad he made the move to Funny Cars. In just his second season in the high-backed racers, he captured his first NASCAR championship. Todd earned the title thanks to six event wins on the season. "This is what you live your whole life for when you start racing Junior Dragster," said Todd. "You hope you'll get to this point, but you go your whole career not knowing if you will." Well, J. R. . . . you did!

PRO STOCK

At 19 years old, **Tanner Gray** was the Pro Stock season winner. That made him the youngest champion in NHRA history! He has only been racing for two seasons, yet he has won 13 times. Gray learned his racing skills early. Both his father and grandfather are pro drag racers.

TOP FUEL

The semifinals at the Toyota Nationals in October decided the season-long finals. First, **Tony Schumacher** lost his semi race. Then **Steve Torrence** roared to victory in his. That gave Torrence enough points to put Schumacher in

PRO STOCK MOTORCYCLE

This division of NHRA racing was the only one with a repeat winner. **Matt Smith** roared past 2017 champion **Eddie Krawiec** in the season's final race to capture his third national championship. In that race at Pomona, Smith also set a new speed record. He drove his high-tech machine at 201.65 miles per hour to capture the flag and the title.

Motorcycle Racing

Webb's No. 2 will be No. 1 in 2020.

2018 MOTOCROSS

Eli Tomac captured his second AMA Motocross title in a row in 2018. He was the first rider to repeat as champion since the great **Ricky Carmichael** ended his run of six straight championships in 2006. Tomac won 15 total motos and eight overall races. He also led the most laps of any rider. Tomac added a pretty nice bonus in October at a three-race Supercross event in Las Vegas. By winning all three of the Vegas races, he took home an additional $1 million!

Eli Tomac churns the dirt!

2019 SUPERCROSS

A new No. 1 plate will start off the 2020 AMA Supercross season. **Cooper Webb** won his first championship in 2019 thanks to seven event victories in his third season on the top 450SX level. Webb capped off the season in the final race at Las Vegas. He needed only to finish 20th, but that's not how this hard-charging young driver rolls. He nearly won, finishing third to earn more than enough points to take home the trophy. In the 250SX categories, **Dylan Ferrandis** won the Western Region, while **Chase Sexton** captured the Eastern title.

Major Champions
OF THE 2000s

TOP FUEL DRAGSTERS

YEAR	DRIVER
2018	Steve Torrence
2017	Brittany Force
2016	Antron Brown
2015	Antron Brown
2014	Tony Schumacher
2013	Shawn Langdon
2012	Antron Brown
2011	Del Worsham
2010	Larry Dixon
2009	Tony Schumacher
2008	Tony Schumacher
2007	Tony Schumacher
2006	Tony Schumacher
2005	Tony Schumacher
2004	Tony Schumacher
2003	Larry Dixon
2002	Larry Dixon
2001	Kenny Bernstein

FUNNY CARS

YEAR	DRIVER
2018	J. R. Todd
2017	Robert Hight
2016	Ron Capps
2015	Del Worsham
2014	Matt Hagan
2013	John Force
2012	Jack Beckman
2011	Matt Hagan
2010	John Force
2009	Robert Hight
2008	Cruz Pedregon
2007	Tony Pedregon
2006	John Force
2005	Gary Scelzi
2004	John Force
2003	Tony Pedregon
2002	John Force
2001	John Force

PRO STOCK CARS

YEAR	DRIVER
2018	Tanner Gray
2017	Bo Butner
2016	Jason Line
2015	Erica Enders-Stevens
2014	Erica Enders-Stevens
2013	Jeg Coughlin, Jr.
2012	Allen Johnson
2011	Jason Line
2010	Greg Anderson
2009	Mike Edwards
2008	Jeg Coughlin, Jr.
2007	Jeg Coughlin, Jr.
2006	Jason Line
2005	Greg Anderson
2004	Greg Anderson
2003	Greg Anderson
2002	Jeg Coughlin, Jr.
2001	Warren Johnson

FORMULA 1

YEAR	DRIVER
2018	Lewis Hamilton
2017	Lewis Hamilton
2016	Nico Rosberg
2015	Lewis Hamilton
2014	Lewis Hamilton
2013	Sebastian Vettel
2012	Sebastian Vettel
2011	Sebastian Vettel
2010	Sebastian Vettel
2009	Jenson Button
2008	Lewis Hamilton
2007	Kimi Räikkönen
2006	Fernando Alonso
2005	Fernando Alonso
2004	Michael Schumacher
2003	Michael Schumacher
2002	Michael Schumacher
2001	Michael Schumacher

INDYCAR SERIES

YEAR	DRIVER
2018	Scott Dixon
2017	Josef Newgarden
2016	Simon Pagenaud
2015	Scott Dixon
2014	Will Power
2013	Scott Dixon
2012	Ryan Hunter-Reay
2011	Dario Franchitti
2010	Dario Franchitti
2009	Dario Franchitti
2008	Scott Dixon
2007	Dario Franchitti
2006	Sam Hornish, Jr.
2005	Dan Wheldon
2004	Tony Kanaan
2003	Scott Dixon
2002	Sam Hornish, Jr.
2001	Sam Hornish, Jr.

AMA SUPERCROSS

YEAR	DRIVER
2019	Cooper Webb
2018	Jason Anderson
2017	Ryan Dungey
2016	Ryan Dungey
2015	Ryan Dungey
2014	Ryan Villopoto
2013	Ryan Villopoto
2012	Ryan Villopoto
2011	Ryan Villopoto
2010	Ryan Dungey
2009	James Stewart, Jr.
2008	Chad Reed
2007	James Stewart, Jr.
2006	Ricky Carmichael
2005	Ricky Carmichael
2004	Chad Reed
2003	Ricky Carmichael
2002	Ricky Carmichael
2001	Ricky Carmichael

AMA MOTOCROSS

YEAR	RIDER (MOTOCROSS)	RIDER (LITES)
2019		
2018	Eli Tomac	Adam Cianciarulo/Zach Osborne
2017	Eli Tomac	Zach Osborne
2016	Ken Roczen	Cooper Webb
2015	Ryan Dungey	Jeremy Martin
2014	Ken Roczen	Jeremy Martin
2013	Ryan Villopoto	Eli Tomac
2012	Ryan Dungey	Blake Baggett
2011	Ryan Villopoto	Dean Wilson
2010	Ryan Dungey	Trey Canard
2009	Chad Reed	Ryan Dungey
2008	James Stewart, Jr.	Ryan Villopoto
2007	Grant Langston	Ryan Villopoto
2006	Ricky Carmichael	Ryan Villopoto
2005	Ricky Carmichael	Ivan Tedesco
2004	Ricky Carmichael	James Stewart, Jr.
2003	Ricky Carmichael	Grant Langston
2002	Ricky Carmichael	James Stewart, Jr.
2001	Ricky Carmichael	Mike Brown

COMING THROUGH!
Canadian Winter X Games skier Alex Beaulieu-Marchand didn't let a few obstacles get in his way during the Ski Slopestyle competition.
He was one of dozens of amazing athletes who showed their skills at Winter X Games. Did your favorites win?

Winter X Games

January in Aspen can mean only one thing: It's time for the X Games! The winter version of the action sports showcase was held in the Colorado resort town for the eighteenth year in a row in 2019. Here are some of the highlights.

Seventh Heaven

Chloe Kim won Snowboard SuperPipe gold in Aspen. That's nothing unusual. The 18-year-old also won gold at the Aspen X Games in 2015, 2016, and 2018. What made this one a bit different is that Kim fell on her first run and entered the second of her three runs in last place. That's unusual! But like all true champions, Kim came through when she needed to most. She was almost flawless with her second run, and moved from last place to first. She soon was on the podium celebrating her seventh career Winter X Games medal.

Chloe Kim soared to gold . . . again!

The Knuckle Huck

A new event with a funny name debuted at the X Games in Aspen. The Knuckle Huck gave nine snowboarders a chance to show off their style and creativity during a 20-minute jam session in which they performed as many tricks as they could fit in. The knuckle is the round bump before a steep landing area. A huck is a free-wheeling trick of the snowboarder's choice. The winner of the inaugural X Games Knuckle Huck was **Fridtjof Sæther Tischendorf** of Norway. We have no idea how to correctly pronounce that name, but you can call him by his nickname: "Fridge"!

Snowboard Pioneer

Trivia time: Who is the winningest snowboarder in history? It's **Kelly Clark**, who announced her retirement at age 35 at the X Games in Aspen. Clark had crashed out of the SuperPipe competition in Aspen in 2018. But no one wanted that to be her last run. So she came back in 2019 for one final celebratory run. Clark's 78 career victories over her 20-year career include an Olympic gold medal and seven X Games titles. More important than all

Ski SuperPipe champ Alex Ferreira: Gold tastes good!

Local Skier Makes Good

It's safe to say that few of the competitors at the X Games had more fans rooting for him than **Alex Ferreira**. That's because the 24-year-old skier was born and raised in Aspen. With his mom, dad, and dozens of family and friends watching from the bottom of the hill, Ferreira nailed his third, and final, run in the Ski SuperPipe to outdistance the competition. He was the first Aspen native since 2010 to win a gold medal.

the wins, however, was the attention that Clark, a snowboarding pioneer, brought to the sport. Her work ethic, intensity, and good cheer helped make snowboarding popular around the world.

2019 WINTER X GAMES CHAMPS

M SKI BIG AIR	**Birk Ruud**
W SKI BIG AIR	**Mathilde Gremaud**
M SKI SLOPESTYLE	**Alex Hall**
W SKI SLOPESTYLE	**Kelly Sildaru**
M SKI SUPERPIPE	**Alex Ferreira**
W SKI SUPERPIPE	**Cassie Sharpe**
SNOW BIKE BEST TRICK	**Rob Adelberg**
SNOW BIKECROSS	**Cody Matechuk**
SNOW BIKECROSS ADAPTIVE	**Mike Schultz**
SNOW BIKECROSS PARA	**Doug Henry**
M SNOWBOARD BIG AIR	**Takeru Otsuka**
W SNOWBOARD BIG AIR	**Laurie Blouin**

SNOWBOARD KNUCKLE HUCK	**Fridtjof Sæther Tischendorf**
M SNOWBOARD SLOPESTYLE	**Mark McMorris**
W SNOWBOARD SLOPESTYLE	**Zoi Sadowski-Synnott**
M SNOWBOARD SUPERPIPE	**Scotty James**
W SNOWBOARD SUPERPIPE	**Chloe Kim**
SNOW HILL CLIMB	**Logan Mead**
SNOWMOBILE FREESTYLE	**Daniel Bodin**
SPECIAL OLYMPICS UNIFIED SNOWBOARD	**Henry Meece-Chris Klug**
X CHALLENGE	**Casey Currie**

Action Notes

Snow Good

In the biathlon, competitors combine skiing with rifle shooting. **Kendall Gretsch** of Illinois did that better than anyone else to win the biathlon at the Para Nordic Skiing World Championships in 2019. Gretsch was perfect with the rifle, and she edged fellow American **Oksana Masters** to win the title in Canada. Gretsch's win built on her history-making performance at the Winter Paralympics in South Korea in 2018. There, she became the first American in either the Olympics or Paralympics to win a gold medal in the biathlon. She also won gold that year in cross-country skiing.

World Surf League

Stephanie Gilmore dominated the World Surf League competition to win the season title for the seventh time in 2018. The Australian star won three of the 10 events. She also finished second twice and third twice to equal fellow Aussie legend **Layne Beachley** for the most career women's world titles. It was an American, though, who opened 2019 atop the standings. Florida native **Caroline Marks** won the season-opening event in Australia. On the men's tour, during the first half of the 2018 season, Brazil's **Gabriel Medina** gave little indication that he was on the way to his second WSL title.

Brazilian surfing star Gabriel Medina shot the curl here on his way to a world championship.

Gretsch made history in the biathlon.

The second half was a different story. He won three of the final five events, including a title-clinching victory in the season-ending Billabong Pipe Masters. Medina used a clutch, perfect-10 ride to clinch his first championship since 2014. In 2019, Medina got off to another slow start. That allowed **Italo Ferreira**, his fellow countryman, to rise to the top of the early season standings.

Freeriders

The Red Bull Rampage is the biggest event for freeride mountain bikers. Freeride is an extreme version of the sport in which competitors make their own paths while combining creativity with technical skill. The Rampage features sandstone ridges and a scary, near-vertical drop down a mountain in the Utah desert. In the fall of 2018, riders spent four days with a two-person crew building their own lines down the mountain. Then they practiced their run for the next four days

before the competition began. Twenty-five-year-old **Brett Rheeder** of Canada used a flat-top backflip to impress the judges—and wow a big crowd—to win the Rampage for the first time.

How I Spent My Summer Vacation

So what does a high school biology teacher do during summer break? Well, if he's **Bryce Carlson** of Cincinnati, Ohio, he spends it rowing across the Atlantic Ocean. In the summer of 2018, Carlson completed a solo row across the Atlantic. It wasn't exactly a relaxing summer. Carlson capsized a dozen times and suffered faulty electronics that made navigation difficult. Still, he made the crossing in a record 38 days, 6 hours, and 49 minutes. That was 15 days faster than the previous fastest mark. Carlson also was the first American to accomplish the feat.

Stroke, stroke, stroke: Carlson hard at work!

GOLF

THE ROAR OF THE TIGER
No longer golf's most dominant player, but still its biggest star, Tiger Woods wowed sports fans everywhere by winning The Masters in April 2019. It was the fifteenth major championship of his career, but his first since 2008.

Major Story

Justin Rose opened 2019 by reclaiming the No. 1 ranking among all golfers in the world. Then **Brooks Koepka** cemented his status as a big-time player in big-time events. Young players such as **Cameron Champ** signaled the next wave of stars. But none of those happenings grabbed the biggest headlines. Instead, the race for story of the year was over early. It came in the spring, when **Tiger Woods** won The Masters for the fifth time. It was his 15th major title in all. Only the legendary **Jack Nicklaus** (with 18) ever won more.

Woods, the best golfer of the last 40 years, had gone through personal and family troubles. Then he had back surgery for the fourth time in April 2017. The man who held the No. 1 ranking in the world longer than any other player ever fell all the way to No. 1,199 by the end of 2017. Still, he rose 1,173 places in 2018 and capped by winning the Tour Championship.

Then came the Masters in 2019. Woods had won the Masters in 1997, 2001, 2002, and 2005. In 2019, he was in a five-way tie for first late in the final round. He took the lead with back-to-back birdies on the 15th and 16th holes. Then he held off three players, including Koepka, to win by one shot. That gave Woods 81 career PGA titles, the second-most ever.

One month later, Woods was the favorite to win the PGA Championship, the season's second major, at Bethpage State Park in New York. But Koepka had other ideas. The 29-year-old American tied the tournament record with a 63 in the opening round. He led from start to finish to win his second consecutive PGA Championship

MEN'S GRAND SLAM EVENTS	
MASTERS	**Tiger Woods**
PGA CHAMPIONSHIP	**Brooks Koepka**
US OPEN	**Gary Woodland**
BRITISH OPEN	**Shane Lowry**

and his fourth major overall. Koepka's victory also rocketed him into the No. 1 ranking.

Koepka was in the hunt yet again at the US Open in June at historic Pebble Beach. But the season's third major went to unheralded **Gary Woodland**. The 35-year-old American drained a long birdie putt to win his first career victory in a major.

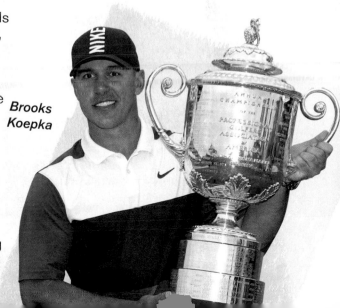

Brooks Koepka

2018 Ryder Cup

Happy Europeans surround the Ryder Cup.

It won 7.5 points from them (a tie earns each player a half point).

Italy's **Francesco Molinari** and Spain's **Sergio Garcia** were the stars for Europe. Molinari was coming off a great season that included a victory at the 2018 British Open. He became the first player ever to win all five of his matches at the Ryder Cup. Garcia, on the other hand, was coming off a down season. Still, he won three of his four matches in France. He also set an all-time record with 25.5 career points in the Ryder Cup.

Meanwhile, **Tiger Woods** and **Phil Mickelson**, the two biggest names on the American roster, went a combined 0–6 in their matches. Ouch!

The Ryder Cup is the biggest team event in golf, and one of the biggest in all of sports. Every two years, teams of golfers from the United States and Europe square off in a competition that began in 1927. The format has been changed over the decades, but the event has never stopped growing in popularity.

In 2018, the sides met at Le Golf National in France. The Europeans won in a rout, 17.5–10.5. The result left Americans to wonder, "What do we have to do to win in Europe?" The US won in Minnesota in 2016, but the debacle in France marked its sixth consecutive road loss in the Ryder Cup. The last time the Americans won on European soil was in 1993.

This one wasn't even close. On Day 1 of the three-day event, Europe swept the four afternoon contests to lead 5–3. By the final day, Europe needed to win only four of the 12 singles matches to clinch the Cup.

RYDER CUP TEAMS

UNITED STATES	EUROPE
Brooks Koepka	Francesco Molinari
Dustin Johnson	Justin Rose
Justin Thomas	Jon Rahm
Patrick Reed	Rory McIlroy
Bubba Watson	Tommy Fleetwood
Jordan Spieth	Tyrrell Hatton
Rickie Fowler	Alex Norén
Webb Simpson	Thorbjorn Olesen
Bryson DeChambeau	Paul Casey
Phil Mickelson	Sergio Garcia
Tiger Woods	Ian Poulter
Tony Finau	Henrik Stenson
Jim Furyk	**Thomas Bjorn**
CAPTAIN	CAPTAIN

Chip Shots

Golf Is Hard!

Local golf pro **Ben DeArmond** was excited to be invited to play in the LECOM Suncoast Classic on the Web.com Tour in February 2019. By the second hole, the excitement wore off! DeArmond hit into the water six times on that par-4 and put a 17 on the scorecard. It was the highest score on any hole in the tour's history. To his credit, DeArmond had a great attitude about it. After finishing his round with a 91, he said, "Everybody has a bad day, a bad hole—even the worst hole of your life. You just have to move on."

Golf Is Easy!

And then there are days when golf doesn't feel so hard at all. In late summer 2018, **Brandt Snedeker** drilled a 20-foot putt on the final hole to complete a round of 59 at the Wyndham Championship in North Carolina. He was just the ninth player ever to break 60 in a PGA Tour event. In June 2019, Snedeker nearly did it again, with a 60 at the Dogwood Invitational.

Mr. 57

Even with a 59 in tournament play, Snedeker had nothing on college golfer **Alex Ross**. In June 2019, the soon-to-be junior at Davidson shot an amazing 57 at the Dogwood Invitational, an amateur tournament in Atlanta. Ross had 13 birdies and an eagle on the par-72 layout.

Remarkably, it came in his second round of the day. Tournament officials decided to play two rounds because bad weather was coming. In Ross' morning round, he shot "only" a 73.

Gold Standard

The rules of golf don't say what golfers must use to mark their ball on the green. Most players use a small coin. Not **Matt Hamilton**, a US Olympic curling champion who played in the Web.com Tour's BMW Charity Pro-Am in June 2019. After hitting close to the cup on one hole, he marked his ball with his 2018 Winter Olympics gold medal!

Snedeker was all smiles after his 59!

LPGA 2019

SECOND-YEAR SENSATION

There was no sophomore slump for South Korean star **Jin Young Ko** in 2019. Ko was the LPGA Rookie of the Year in 2018, when she posted 13 top-10 finishes in 25 starts. But that was just a taste of what was to come. Ko opened 2019 by finishing second at the ISPS Handa Women's Australian Open, then tied for third at the HSBC Women's World Championship two weeks later. In March, she won the Bank of Hope Founders Cup and tied for second at the Kia Classic. Then she capped her amazing run by winning the ANA Inspiration

284.5

That's the LPGA record (in yards) for driving distance in a season. Sweden's **Karen Sjodin** set the mark in 2006. **Anne van Dam** of the Netherlands was on pace to top the record in 2019. She entered the summer at 284.9.

in April. It was her first major championship. What was Ko's secret? It was to focus only on the moment. "I'm thinking just shot by shot," she said. "I don't like thinking about the future. Nobody knows about my future or your future."

SIXTH SENSE

More than two decades ago, 20-year-old South Korean **Se Ri Pak** won the 1998 US Women's Open as a rookie. That victory inspired many of Pak's fellow countrywomen to follow in her footsteps on the LPGA Tour. One of the latest stars from South Korea is **Jeongeun Lee6**. At 23 in 2019, she won her first major championship when she edged three other golfers by two shots to win the US Women's Open in South Carolina. It was the ninth time since Pak's victory that a South Korean golfer won the US Women's Open. The 23-year-old Jeongeun Lee6 began her pro career on the LPGA of Korea

Jeongeun Lee6

LPGA star Madsen gets help from a lemon!

New Jersey, she drained a 20-foot putt for eagle at the par-5 18th. The crowd went wild, but it wasn't only the fans who were excited. "I got chills," Thompson said, "The hair on my arms was sticking up once I made that putt." Thompson beat Lee6 by one shot.

Tour in 2016. When she started out, five other players on the tour also were named Jeongeun Lee. That's why she includes the unusual "6" in her name.

WEDGE GAME
Athletes have all kinds of ways to deal with pressure. It's safe to say that LPGA golfer **Nanna Koerstz Madsen** utilizes one of the more unusual ones. The native of Denmark bites into a lemon wedge. That's right. Whenever the going gets a little too intense, she grabs one of the wedges that her caddie carefully wraps for her before every round. Now, if you've ever bit into a lemon, you're probably thinking, "Yuck!" It's so sour that you can't think of anything else. Which is exactly the trick for Madsen. "Well, it's just if I get nervous or too angry or something, it's just to take my mind off that stuff. So, yeah, I bite a lemon."

FANTASTIC FINISH
Lexi Thompson has been one of the top American golfers ever since she turned pro at the age of 15 in 2010. In June 2019, she posted her 11th LPGA Tour victory in dramatic fashion. Tied for the lead on the last hole of the ShopRite LPGA Classic in

Thompson has one win each year since 2013.

WOMEN'S GRAND SLAM EVENTS

ANA INSPIRATION	**Jin Young Ko**
US WOMEN'S OPEN	**Jeongeun Lee6**
WOMEN'S PGA CHAMPIONSHIP	**Hannah Green**
THE EVIAN CHAMPIONSHIP	**Jin Young Ko**
WOMEN'S BRITISH OPEN	**Hinako Shibuno**

The Majors

In golf, some tournaments are known as the majors. They're the most important events of the year on the men's and women's pro tours. (There are four men's majors and five women's majors.) Among the men, **Jack Nicklaus** holds the record for the most all-time wins in the majors. **Patty Berg** won more majors than any other women's player.

MEN'S

	MASTERS	US OPEN	BRITISH OPEN	PGA CHAMP.	TOTAL
Jack **NICKLAUS**	6	4	3	5	**18**
Tiger **WOODS**	5	3	3	4	**15**
Walter **HAGEN**	0	2	4	5	**11**
Ben **HOGAN**	2	4	1	2	**9**
Gary **PLAYER**	3	1	3	2	**9**
Tom **WATSON**	2	1	5	0	**8**
Bobby **JONES**	0	4	3	0	**7**
Arnold **PALMER**	4	1	2	0	**7**
Gene **SARAZEN**	1	2	1	3	**7**
Sam **SNEAD**	3	0	1	3	**7**
Harry **VARDON**	0	1	6	0	**7**

RYDER CUP RESULTS

Note: The current format of the United States versus Europe began in 1979.

YEAR	WINNING TEAM	SCORE	YEAR	WINNING TEAM	SCORE
2018	**EUROPE**	17.5–10.5	1997	**EUROPE**	14.5–13.5
2016	**UNITED STATES**	17–11	1995	**EUROPE**	14.5–13.5
2014	**EUROPE**	16.5–11.5	1993	**UNITED STATES**	15–13
2012	**EUROPE**	14.5–13.5	1991	**UNITED STATES**	14.5–13.5
2010	**EUROPE**	14.5–13.5	1989	**TIE**	14–14
2008	**UNITED STATES**	16.5–11.5	1987	**EUROPE**	15–13
2006	**EUROPE**	18.5–9.5	1985	**EUROPE**	16.5–11.5
2004	**EUROPE**	18.5–9.5	1983	**UNITED STATES**	14.5–13.5
2002	**EUROPE**	15.5–12.5	1981	**UNITED STATES**	18.5–9.5
1999	**UNITED STATES**	14.5–13.5	1979	**UNITED STATES**	17–11

WOMEN'S

	LPGA	USO	BO	ANA	EV	MAUR	TH	WES	TOTAL
Patty **BERG**	0	1	0	0	0	0	7	7	15
Mickey **WRIGHT**	4	4	0	0	0	0	2	3	13
Louise **SUGGS**	1	2	0	0	0	0	4	4	11
Annika **SÖRENSTAM**	3	3	1	3	0	0	0	0	10
Babe **ZAHARIAS**	0	3	0	0	0	0	3	4	10
Betsy **RAWLS**	2	4	0	0	0	0	0	2	8
Juli **INKSTER**	2	2	0	2	0	1	0	0	7
Inbee **PARK**	3	2	1	1	0	0	0	0	7
Karrie **WEBB**	1	2	1	2	0	1	0	0	7

KEY: LPGA = LPGA Championship, USO = US Open, BO = British Open, ANA = ANA Inspiration, EV = Evian Championship, MAUR = du Maurier (1979–2000), TH = Titleholders (1937–1972), WES = Western Open (1937–1967)

PGA TOUR CAREER EARNINGS*

1.	Tiger Woods	$118,663,768
2.	Phil Mickelson	$90,513,535
3.	Vijay Singh	$71,216,128
4.	Jim Furyk	$70,916,515
5.	Dustin Johnson	$61,518,538
6.	Justin Rose	$52,950,988
7.	Adam Scott	$52,647,434
8.	Matt Kuchar	$49,874,171
9.	Sergio Garcia	$49,780,473
10.	Ernie Els	$49,264,449

LPGA TOUR CAREER EARNINGS*

1.	Annika Sörenstam	$22,573,192
2.	Karrie Webb	$20,264,869
3.	Cristie Kerr	$19,745,104
4.	Inbee Park	$14,898,924
5.	Lorena Ochoa	$14,863,331

*Through June 2018

MATT KUCHAR

Two wins and two second-place finishes early in the 2019 season helped Kuchar leap into the all-time top 10 for the first time. He had earned more than $6 million through June 2019, already his highest single-season total ever. It was quite a rebound for a player who had not won a tournament since 2014. He came close in 2017, finishing second in the US Open. The native of Florida is also a four-time member of the United States Ryder Cup team.

TENNIS

SPEAK SOFTLY AND CARRY A BIG RACKET
Naomi Osaka rose to No. 1 in the world rankings with her title at the Australian Open in 2019. The 21-year-old is quiet off the court but uses raw power to overwhelm opponents on it.

2019 Women's Tennis

For years, the tennis world has seen **Naomi Osaka** coming. The native of Japan (and resident of the United States since she was three) played her first match on the ITF Women's Circuit the day she turned 14. By 16, she could hit 100 mile-per-hour forehands. Soon she was serving the ball at 125 miles per hour! It was just a matter of time until Osaka put it all together.

That happened in 2018 when she matched mental success with physical talent. She stopped getting down on herself and cut her number of errors. The result? Her first title at a Grand Slam event, the US Open, late in the season.

The 21-year-old entered 2019 ranked No. 4 in world, and was one of 11 players with a chance to rise to No. 1 at the season's first major, the Australian Open. When she beat the Czech Republic's **Petra Kvitová** in the final, she became the first Asian player ever to hold the top spot in the women's world rankings.

Ashleigh Barty failed in her attempt to win that Grand Slam event in her home country. However, she did become the first Australian woman in more than a decade to make it to the quarterfinals. Then, several months later, she entered the 2019 French

Aussie Barty won her first major title.

Open as the No. 8 seed in the tournament. This time, she swept through to the finals, where she beat **Marketa Vondrousova** of the Czech Republic to win her first Grand Slam title. Barty became the first Australian woman in 46 years to win the French Open. By late June, she passed Osaka to become the first world No. 1 Australian since 1976.

Barty's win at Roland-Garros made her only the fifth two-time winner on the 2019 WTA Tour. (She also won at Miami in March.) The first 27 events on the schedule produced 22 different winners. **Kiki Bertens**, Petra Kvitová, **Karolína Plíšková**, and **Dayana Yastremska** joined Barty as multiple winners over the first half of the year.

2019 WOMEN'S GRAND SLAMS

AUSTRALIAN OPEN	**Naomi Osaka**
FRENCH OPEN	**Ashleigh Barty**
WIMBLEDON	**Simona Halep**
US OPEN	_____

2019 Men's Tennis

The start of the men's tennis season in 2019 brought the same question as the last several seasons. Would this finally be the year a group of new stars grabbed the spotlight from dominant veterans? Well, no . . . not yet. **Novak Djokovic** (32 years old), **Rafael Nadal** (33), and **Roger Federer** (37) maintained their grip on the top rungs of the tennis ladder.

It started when Djokovic and Nadal met in January in the final of the first major championship of the season, the Australian Open. Djokovic overpowered Nadal in straight sets to win his 15th Grand Slam event. That moves him to third all time (behind Federer and Nadal, of course!). It was the Serbian star's record seventh Australian Open title.

The next major was the French Open in June. It looked as if Djokovic and Nadal were headed for another finals showdown, but Djokovic dropped a five-set thriller to Austrian **Dominic Thiem** in a semifinal. Nadal then cruised past Thiem in four sets in the final to win title No. 12 on the clay courts of Roland-Garros. That is twice as many French Opens as any other winner.

Federer lost to Nadal in the semifinals. The Swiss superstar had won early season

Nadal contined as the master of clay courts.

tournaments in both Dubai and Miami. More than halfway through the 2019 season, that left Djokovic, Nadal, and Federer still holding down the top three spots in the world rankings. Thiem (25 years old), **Alexander Zverev** (22), and **Stefanos Tsitsipas** (20) were among the young stars trying to make a move up.

After the French Open, one national tennis writer ranked Nadal's 12 French Open wins. (The 2019 victory was No. 1.) The reporter said that, at 33, Nadal may not have very many more chances left to add to his total. Still, if 2019 taught us anything, it's that the old guys (still) rule.

2019 MEN'S GRAND SLAMS

AUSTRALIAN OPEN	**Novak Djokovic**
FRENCH OPEN	**Rafael Nadal**
WIMBLEDON	**Novak Djokovic**
US OPEN	_____

Tennis Notes

The Pride of Greece ▶▶▶

No Greek player ever ranked among the top 10 men in the world until **Stefanos Tsitsipas** reached No. 6 early in 2019. The 20-year-old from Athens, who speaks English, Greek, and Russian, and vlogs on YouTube when he's not on the court, reached the Australian Open semifinals early in the season.

Two-Sport Star

Australian **Ashleigh Barty** won the 2019 French Open (see page 157) even while keeping one eye on the Cricket World Cup. That's because Barty once turned in her tennis racket for a cricket bat. In 2015, she played for the Brisbane Heat of the Women's Big Bash League (WBBL). Barty

played one season in the WBBL, then returned to pro tennis in 2016.

◀◀◀ Big Late Win

Rising star **Elina Svitolina** of the Ukraine won the 2018 WTA Finals event for the first time. She beat American **Sloane Stephens**. It was the ninth finals win in a row for Svitolina, wrapping up her best season ever.

Spreading the Wealth

Even though the Big Three continued to dominate the top events in men's tennis in 2019 (see page 158), the men's ATP Tour may never have had so many good players from top to bottom. A 19-tournament stretch during the 2018 and 2019 seasons produced 19 different winners.

Grand Slams

ALL-TIME GRAND SLAM CHAMPIONSHIPS (MEN)

	AUSTRALIAN	FRENCH	WIMBLEDON	US OPEN	TOTAL
Roger **FEDERER**	6	1	8	5	**20**
Rafael **NADAL**	1	12	2	3	**18**
Novak **DJOKOVIC**	7	1	5	3	**16**
Pete **SAMPRAS**	2	0	7	5	**14**
Roy **EMERSON**	6	2	2	2	**12**
Björn **BORG**	0	6	5	0	**11**
Rod **LAVER**	3	2	4	2	**11**
Bill **TILDEN**	0	0	3	7	**10**
Andre **AGASSI**	4	1	1	2	**8**
Jimmy **CONNORS**	1	0	2	5	**8**
Ivan **LENDL**	2	3	0	3	**8**
Fred **PERRY**	1	1	3	3	**8**
Ken **ROSEWALL**	4	2	0	2	**8**

BJÖRN BORG

For a player who never won either the Australian or US Opens, Sweden's **Björn Borg** won a lot of Grand Slams! Not until **Rafael Nadal** came along had anyone won more French Opens. He was also the king of Wimbledon until **Pete Sampras** and later **Roger Federer** topped his mark. He also helped Sweden win the 1975 Davis Cup. He was known for his court-covering speed and his long, flowing hair. Borg retired at the age of 26 in 1983. He was later elected to the International Tennis Hall of Fame.

ALL-TIME GRAND SLAM CHAMPIONSHIPS (WOMEN)

	AUSTRALIAN	FRENCH	WIMBLEDON	US OPEN	TOTAL
Margaret Smith **COURT**	11	5	3	5	**24**
Serena **WILLIAMS**	7	3	7	6	**23**
Steffi **GRAF**	4	6	7	5	**22**
Helen Wills **MOODY**	0	4	8	7	**19**
Chris **EVERT**	2	7	3	6	**18**
Martina **NAVRATILOVA**	3	2	9	4	**18**
Billie Jean **KING**	1	1	6	4	**12**
Maureen **CONNOLLY**	1	2	3	3	**9**
Monica **SELES**	4	3	0	2	**9**
Suzanne **LENGLEN**	0	2*	6	0	**8**
Molla Bjurstedt **MALLORY**	0	0	0	8	**8**

*Also won four French titles before 1925; in those years, the tournament was open only to French nationals.

Suzanne Lenglen

The stylish and forward-thinking French star dominated European tennis in the 1920s. She was an Olympic gold medalist in 1920 and the top-ranked player in the world from 1921 to 1926. She rolled up an incredible mark of 34 Grand Slam titles in singles, doubles, and mixed doubles. From 1919 to 1926, she was defeated only once in a singles match. She got almost as much attention for her tennis gear. Lenglen was the first woman to play in calf-length skirts and short-sleeve tops. Her headband became a big part of her "look," as well. She was one of the first women to play as a professional and became a worldwide celebrity. Sadly, she died at the age of 39 of a blood disease, but her tennis career made her a legend.

SUDDEN STARS

PETE ALONSO
NY METS

Talk about persistence! Pete Alonso was not drafted by a Major League team out of high school. So he kept slugging at the University of Florida and was drafted by the New York Mets in 2016. In 2018, he whacked 36 homers in the minors. In 2019, he set a new MLB rookie record with 20 homers by June 1. He also broke the Mets team rookie record and then won the MLB Home Run Derby!

EFRAÍN ÁLVAREZ

LA GALAXY

Young stars are not unusual in soccer, but Álvarez still stands out. He was only 16 when he made his debut in February 2019 with the Los Angeles Galaxy. Oh, and he also had an assist in his first pro game! Later in the summer, he led Mexico to the CONCACAF U-17 championship. With time still to grow and learn, Álvarez will be adding more highlights very soon.

LUKA DONČIĆ
DALLAS MAVERICKS

Dončić celebrated the night before his 20th birthday by pouring in 26 points for the Dallas Mavericks in a win over the Pacers. It was another highlight for this young superstar. Born in Slovenia, Dončić has been a pro since he was 16, playing for Real Madrid in Spain. In 2018, he was the EuroLeague MVP and helped Real win the title. The Mavs chose him with the third overall pick and he didn't disappoint. An all-around star, he averaged 21.2 points in 2018–19 and was named NBA Rookie of the Year.

COCO GAUFF
WTA

What a start! Almost out of nowhere, American tennis player Coco Gauff became one of the biggest stories in her sport. She qualified for Wimbledon in 2019 at the age of 15! That made her the youngest player in the Open (pro tennis) era to do that for a Grand Slam event. Then she won her first match over one of her idols, Venus Williams! Gauff made it to the fourth round before losing, but it sure was a great beginning!

JIN YOUNG KO
LPGA

Talk about a fast rise to the top. In 2017, Jin Young Ko was not even a member of the LPGA Tour. Her first tournament victory that year earned her a spot on the 2018 schedule. She took full advantage. The Korean native led the tour in lowest average score and was named rookie of the year. She kept it up, and by mid-2019 was the No. 1-ranked player in the world.

PHILLIP LINDSAY
DENVER BRONCOS

When a college football star is not drafted by an NFL team, he can choose to sulk and be sad. Or he can choose to work harder. Lindsay worked harder. The Denver native battled his way through Broncos tryout camps to earn a spot on the team. He ran for 107 yards in his second game and became a regular. Lindsay became the second undrafted runner ever to top 1,000 yards. He also scored 9 TDs. No more tryouts for him!

ALYSA LIU

As the scores went up, Alysa Liu's mouth opened into a giant O. She and her coach could barely believe what they were seeing. But it was true: Liu's numbers after the free skate at the 2019 US Figure Skating Championships were the highest of the event. At only 13 years old, she became the youngest national champ in American skating history. She was also the first to land two triple axels in one event.

ELIAS PETTERSSON
VANCOUVER CANUCKS

This native of Sweden was the fifth overall pick in the 2018 NHL Draft, but his rookie success went beyond even what he expected. Pettersson led all first-year players in goals, asissts, and points, along with power-play and game-winning goals. Other rookies got more headlines, but once the pucks hit the ice, Pettersson got the most. After the season, he was named the NHL Rookie of the Year.

AUSTIN RILEY
ATLANTA BRAVES

Riley thought he had a shot to join the Braves in 2019, but then the team signed a veteran at third base, Riley's position. But Riley swung such a hot bat, the team found him a new position in left field. He hit a homer in his first game and by his 20th, he had eight more and was hitting .320. Riley was expected to be good . . . but his early success surprised many fans.

A'JA WILSON
LAS VEGAS ACES

Wilson is used to winning, which is what everyone wants to do in Las Vegas. This high-scoring center does her winning on the court in the WNBA. Wilson had a great first season in 2018, earning Rookie of the Year honors. She was in the league top ten in both rebounds and points per game. She's a proven winner, too; she led South Carolina to the 2017 NCAA championship.

OTHER SPORTS

SOARING SIMONE
American gymnast Simone Biles flies through the air as she competes in the World Gymnastics Championships. The young star became the first woman ever to win four straight all-around titles. Read more about her feats and check out some other games and events that deserve a place in our Year in Sports!

Esports

Biggest Upset Ever?: During the League of Legends Midseason Invitational, fans watching online and live at the Hanoi, Vietnam, stadium could not believe what they were seeing. In the semifinal, the North American Team Liquid had jumped out to a two-game lead over China's world-champion Invictus Game. Surely this could not continue. Most experts had said that Liquid could not even win one game, let alone two. But the shocks kept coming, as Liquid's great use of Skarner in the fourth game clinched the match. Was this the biggest upset in League of Legends history? Liquid lost in the final to G2, but their place in history was set in the semis.

Stick With It!: Shanghai Dragons had a very tough first season in Overwatch League in 2018, losing all 40 of their matches . . . in a row! They lost two more to start 2019 before finally ending up on top. Showing that persistence pays, Shanghai beat Boston 3–1 in a February duel.

Big Money: The richest prize in esports history awaited the winner of the huge DOTA International. For the first time, the event was held in China. After nearly two weeks of competition, one emerged on top and took home a new record prize. Since this ended after we printed:

Who won?_____

How much did they earn?_____

Team Liquid made it to the Midseason after winning here in St. Louis.

Cricket World Cup

Just as esports draws fans from around the world, so does the sport of cricket. Some experts think there might be as many as 2.5 billion fans of this ball-and-bat sport. In the summer of 2019, a whole lot of them were tuned in to the Cricket World Cup, held in England and Wales. The event ended with a game that will be talked about for decades.

The top ten teams in the world gathered to play head-to-head "one-day international" matches. Some cricket matches can last five days, so the World Cup had to use the shorter format . . . or else it would take months to finish! Australia entered as the defending champ and, but cricket-crazy countries like Bangladesh and Pakistan were hoping for upsets.

After more than 40 matches, Pakistan had the same number of points and wins as New Zealand. The next tiebreaker was called the net-run rule and Pakistan's total there was just below the Kiwis. By the slimmest of margins, New Zealand joined England, India, and Australia in the semifinals.

England used the power of homefield advantage and surprised the powerful Aussies in one semifinal. They got top batter **David Warner** very quickly. Australia put up a low (for them) 223 runs. In the other semi, India batted second but its early batters were bowled

Warner was a top batter, but not a champ.

out quickly. They could not recover and New Zealand held on for a place in the final.

The championship started with New Zealand putting up 241 runs. On the very last ball of its turn at bat, England scored to tie the score! In the Super Over, England matched New Zealand's 15 runs and won the tiebreaker for having hit the most boundaries in the game. Wow!

Maximum Security (left) won. Then it didn't, and Country House did!

Triple Crown Races

The Kentucky Derby has seen some amazing finishes in its 145-year history. The 2019 race featured an all-time first. **Maximum Security** led for the whole race and galloped through the finish line in first place. The jockey of rival **Country House** complained that the winner had broken the rules. After more than 20 minutes of studying video, race officials agreed. For the first time ever at the Derby, the winning horse was disqualified for illegally getting in the way of other horses. Country House was declared the winner after finishing behind Maximum Security. It was a tough ending, but experts agreed that it was the right decision.

Another horse that was blocked in the Derby got its revenge in the Preakness Stakes. **War of Will** lost in Kentucky, but roared to the Preakness lead on its final turn. It was the first Triple Crown win for jockey **Tyler Gaffalione**. An odd note: Jockey **John Velazquez** was thrown from a horse named **Bodexpress** right at the start. The horse ran nearly the whole race without a jockey!

No horse captured all three legs of the Triple Crown, but one trainer almost did. Mark Cresse had led War of Will in the Preakness. In the Beltmon Stakes, his horse **Sir Winston** was the upset winner.

Lacrosse

NATIONAL LACROSSE LEAGUE

At the 2019 NLL Finals, defense was the word of the day in Game 1. The Calgary Roughnecks and Buffalo Bandits were tied at only 2–2 at halftime. Both teams' goalies were outstanding. In the second half, though, **Dane Dobie** of Calgary had a hat trick. The Roughnecks moved to a 9–4 lead and Buffalo could not catch up. In Game 2, played in Calgary, the two teams tied at 13–13 to force overtime. Roughnecks goalie **Christian Del Bianco** came up big, making two amazing saves. That opened the door for his teammate **Rhys Duch** to score the game-winner. That gave Calgary its first NLL title since 2009.

MAJOR LEAGUE LACROSSE

In the 2018 MLL championship game, things did not look good for the Denver Outlaws. During the second quarter, Denver trailed the Dallas Rattlers 9–6. Then a four-goal outburst gave Denver the halftime lead. "Those four goals at the end of the half gave us a good feeling going into halftime," said Outlaws coach **BJ O'Hara**. In the second half, they kept that good feeling going. **Matt Kavanagh** led the way with four goals and five assists. Denver had not beaten Dallas in 2018, but they saved their best for last. The Outlaws carried home their third Steinfeld Trophy with a 16–12 win.

The Roughnecks celebrated after becoming the 2019 National Lacrosse League champs.

Gymnastics

No Olympics? No problem! The world's best gymnasts gathered at the annual World Championships in Doha, Qatar, in late 2018. As she did in the Olympics two years before, American star **Simone Biles** shined the brightest. She won the World all-around championship for the fourth time. She is the first gymnast ever to reach that total!

Biles had to overcome some mistakes to win. She is normally near-perfect, but in Qatar she fell in the vault and balance beam during the all-around. Despite those problems, her score was 1.693 points higher than any other gymnast. That was the biggest margin for any of her four world titles. **Mai Murakami** of Japan earned the silver for second place.

After winning the all-around, Biles earned a gold medal in the floor exercises and in the vault. She captured a silver medal for second place in the uneven bars and a bronze in the beam. Add up all that hardware and Biles has now earned 20 World Championship medals in her career! That is tied for the most all-time with **Svetlana Khorkina** of Russia. Biles hoped to top that record in the 2019 event as she prepared for the 2020 Summer Olympics in Tokyo.

Biles was not the only American star at the Worlds. Biles led the United States to the gold medal in the team competition. She got a lot of help there from **Morgan Hurd**, the surprise winner of the 2018 United States championship. Hurd not only finished third to Biles in the all-around at Worlds, but won a silver in floor exercises.

Morgan Hurd

A MASS OF MEDALS

Simone Biles is going to need a new room for her growing pile of gymnastic medals. Here's what she has won so far, through the 2018 World Championships. And this does not include the many medals she has won at the junior level or in smaller national competitions! (Note: She took 2017 off to rest and get ready for more events!)

2018 World Championships	2015 World Championships	2014 World Championships	2013 World Championships	2016 Summer Olympics
TEAM ●	TEAM ●	TEAM ●	ALL-AROUND ●	TEAM ●
ALL-AROUND ●	ALL-AROUND ●	ALL-AROUND ●	FLOOR EXERCISE ●	ALL-AROUND ●
VAULT ●	BALANCE BEAM ●	BALANCE BEAM ●	VAULT ●	VAULT ●
FLOOR EXERCISE ●	FLOOR EXERCISE ●	FLOOR EXERCISE ●	BALANCE BEAM ●	FLOOR EXERCISE ●
UNEVEN BARS ●	VAULT ●	VAULT ●		BALANCE BEAM ●
BALANCE BEAM ●				

KEY   Gold = ●   Silver = ●   Bronze = ●

MEN'S CHAMPIONSHIPS

American **Sam Mikulak** (right) earned his first medal at a World Championships. He came in third in the high bar to earn a bronze. Mikulak's medal was the biggest highlight of a very solid meet for the American men. They finished fourth in the team event, just missing a medal by 1.75 points. (If you think that was close, check this out: China beat Russia for the team gold by a razor-thin 0.049 points!) Mikulak also finished fifth in the men's all-around, the highest by an American since 2012. He also just missed two more medals by finishing fourth in pommel horse and parallel bars. Teammate **Yul Moldauer** also barely missed a bronze in floor exercise.

Winter Sports

2019 World Cup Skiing

Skiing's World Cup lasts for a long and demanding season. Racers fly around the world to take on the toughest mountain courses. It takes great all-around skill and endurance to succeed. In 2019, **Mikaela Shiffrin** of the United States continued to be the best female skier in the world. She won the overall women's World Cup for the third time in a row. Her best events are the slalom and giant slalom, and she was the World Cup champ in those events. She also won the Super-G. Her final total of 2,204 points was nearly 1,000 more than second-place **Petra Vlhova** of Slovakia.

At the World Championships, Shiffrin also became the first person to win four straight titles in one type of racing when she captured the slalom. She also added the Super-G title for good measure! With the retirement of American World Cup legend **Lindsey Vonn** (see box at right), Shiffrin moves in as the top female skier in the world.

In the men's World Cup, fans watched familiar faces win again. Austria's **Marcel Hirscher** won his amazing eighth straight World Cup overall title. That is far and away the best streak ever. A big reason was his season championships in both the slalom and giant slalom. **Henrik Kristoffersen** of Norway won his second giant slalom in a row, while **Beat Fuez** went back-to-back in the downhill. **Alexis Pinterault** earned his fifth championship in the Combined event. **Dominik Paris** of Italy was a first-time champ in the Super-G.

Can Shiffrin beat Vonn's record some day?

Goodbye, Lindsey!

The greatest female skier of all time finished her last race in 2019. American **Lindsey Vonn** retired with enough hardware to fill a dozen trophy cases. Vonn was the overall World Cup champion four times. She won 82 World Cup races, the most ever by a woman and second only to Sweden's great **Ingemar Stenmark**. Among her three Olympic medals was a gold in the 2010 downhill. Vonn's powerful skiing and ability to bounce back from injury made her a world superstar. It was all those injuries that finally forced her off her skis.

2019 FIGURE SKATING WORLD CHAMPIONSHIPS

Figure skating is hard enough without everyone watching rooting for you to fall. American star **Nathan Chen** (left) skated after Japan's **Yuzuru Hanyu** at the 2019 World Championships. Did we mention the event was IN Japan?! Chen came through like the champion he is. He put on a marvelous show, nailing jump after jump. He got high marks for his beautiful style, too. When the scores went up, he was the world champion for the second year in a row. More good news for the American team: **Vincent Zhou** earned the bronze medal. It was the first time since 1996 that two American men earned World Championship medals.

Russian skater **Alina Zagitova** was a surprise winner at the 2018 Winter Olympics. So it was not a huge surprise that she won her first World Championship in 2019. Only 16, she had the top scores in the short program and free skate. **Brandie Tennell** finished seventh to be the top American.

China's **Sui Wenjing** and **Han Cong** won the gold in the pairs event. In ice dancing, France's **Gabriella Papadakis** and **Guillame Cizeron** made it four world titles in a row.

Toward the end of his long walk, Colin O'Brady's sled was smaller and lighter.

Offbeat Sports

Not every sport or competition makes the highlights on TV or online. We've combed the edges of the sports world to bring you these cool sports stories!

A Long, Hard Race: If you're going to race someone for 50 days, you would think you might pick somewhere easier to travel than the bottom of the world! But Antarctica is just where **Colin O'Brady** and **Louis Rudd** went to see who could cross the huge, icy continent first. The trick was they would both go without any help. That is, they had to carry everything they needed to survive. No one could fly in and give them aid. The two battled ice, wind, cold, hunger, and very sore feet for nearly two months. O'Brady ended up finishing first. On the final leg, he covered 77 miles in 32 hours without a break. The two men covered the 921 miles in 50 days, pulling sleds loaded with gear and food.

Skydiving . . . Indoors?: Huge fans blast high-speed air into a huge tube. Climb in and you can "fly"! These indoor skydiving sites have popped up worldwide. They are usually for tourists and semi-daredevils, but of course, some folks are better than ever. A worldwide series of events tests the indoor flying skills of experts. In the wind-whipped tube, athletes fly in formations, perform freestyle moves, or take part in relay races. Make sure to check out videos!

So Close: An American came close to winning the World Chess Championship for the first time in 46 years. **Fabiano Caruana** was born in Miami but trained for chess in Italy.

He made the final against three-time defending champion **Magnus Carlsen** of Norway. Caruana made it hard, "drawing" (tying) 12 straight games. In the faster-paced overtime games, Carlsen surged ahead and won. The US will have to wait at least another year. The last US champ remains **Bobby Fischer**, who won in 1972.

to take the elevators back down). The 2018 world champion was **Piotr Lobodzinskí**, who won his fifth title. Australia's **Suzy Walsham** did him two better, winning her seventh VWC championship. Races in 2019 were held in Japan, Singapore, France, and the United States. Think about that next time you walk up the stairs!

Where's the Backboard?:

That's probably what you'd say if you got a look at a netball game. Netball is like basketball, but there is no backboard, just a rim and a net. Seven-player teams, usually women, run and pass on a wooden court, just like basketball. Only two players from each team can shoot, however. More than 60 countries have national teams. The best faced off in the 2019 Netball World Cup, held in England. This ended after our deadline, so go online and check out videos of this cool sport. Maybe you can even start a netball club at your school!

2019 Netball World Cup Champions:
New Zealand

That's a LOT of Steps:

Fitness fans count their steps on fancy watches, but most of those steps are on flat ground. Really fit people count steps as they walk UP them. For more than a decade, the Vertical World Circuit has hosted a series of races UP very tall buildings! Eleven skyscrapers around the world fill their stairways with very fit runners who race to the top (they get

Netball athletes go for the hoop!

NCAA Women 2018–19

FIELD HOCKEY: North Carolina

North Carolina and Maryland are familiar foes in this sport. The Tar Heels and the Terrapins met in the championship game for the seventh time in November 2018. Each side had three wins in title-game matchups until North Carolina broke through with a 2–0 victory in this one. **Erin Matson's** 20th goal of the season capped the scoring as the Tar Heels closed a perfect season at 23–0.

GOLF: Duke

Move over, Coach K. Everybody knows about Duke's amazing men's basketball team. Legendary coach

Mike Krzyzewski has led the Blue Devils to five national championships. But he's got nothing on coach **Dan Brooks** and the school's women's golf team. The Blue Devils won their seventh national title in that sport in the spring of 2019. Duke rallied for a 3–2 win over Atlantic Coast Conference rival Wake Forest in the final. The Blue Devils and Demon Deacons went extra holes in three of the five matches, with Duke winning two of them to take the title.

FENCING: Columbia

Chalk up another one for the Ivy League, which but has dominated NCAA fencing. In 2019, Columbia won the combined

A Columbia fencer (left) scores a point in the championship final.

Spike! UCLA smashes one against USC.

BEACH VOLLEYBALL: UCLA

It seems like it's beach weather all year round in Los Angeles, so it's no surprise the national champion in this sport came from there . . . for the fourth time in the four-year history of the event. **Abby Van Winkle** and **Zana Muno** won the clinching match as the Bruins swept cross-town rival USC to win the title for the second year in a row. The Trojans were the champs in 2016 and 2017.

INDOOR TRACK: Arkansas

The 2019 Indoor Track Championships were a Southeastern Conference affair. Arkansas took the women's title while Florida won on the men's side. The Razorbacks came from behind over the final four events to overtake runner-up USC by 11 points. **Lexi Jacobus** started the rally by soaring 15 feet and 1.5 inches to win the pole vault.

women's and men's sport for the sixteenth time in its history. It was the fifth time in the last 14 seasons that an Ivy League school topped the nation. The Lions took the lead early in this four-day event and never let up. Columbia's **Anne Cebula** won the women's épée individual title. **Sylvie Binder** was the foil champion.

CROSS COUNTRY: Colorado

Colorado senior **Dani Jones** capped her college career with a furious finishing kick on the final straightaway of the NCAA title race in the fall of 2018. That sent her past leader **Weini Kelati** of New Mexico to win the individual title. But Jones also had plenty of help as Colorado easily outdistanced the favored Lobos to win the team title. Five more of her teammates placed among the top 30 finishers overall.

Other National Champions

BOWLING: **Stephen F. Austin**
GYMNASTICS: **Oklahoma**
ICE HOCKEY: **Wisconsin**
LACROSSE: **Maryland**
SOCCER: **Florida State**
SOFTBALL: **UCLA**
SWIMMING AND DIVING: **Stanford**
TENNIS: **Stanford**
TRACK AND FIELD (OUTDOOR): **Arkansas**
VOLLEYBALL: **Stanford**
WATER POLO: **Stanford**

NCAA Men 2018–19

Akron goalie Ben Lundt came up big!

The score in the deciding set was 25–23. It was the second consecutive title for Long Beach State, which won the championship on its home court.

SOCCER: Maryland

Akron's **Ben Lundt** was spectacular in goal all night, but Maryland's **Amar Sejdic** put a penalty kick past him in the 57th minute. It was the only scoring in the Terrapins' 1–0 win in the College Cup final in Santa Barbara, California, in December 2018. Maryland keeper **Dayne St. Clair** posted a shutout for his side. The Terrapins won their fourth national title, but their first in 10 years.

GYMNASTICS: Stanford

Second-ranked Stanford ended top-rated Oklahoma's streak of 121 meet wins—including four NCAA titles—by coming from behind in the 2019 final. **Brody Malone** keyed the Cardinal's victory. He became just the third freshman ever to win the all-around title. The victory marked Stanford's 120th NCAA team championship in all sports—the most of any school in history.

TENNIS: Texas

Texas has a long and storied history in athletics. The Longhorns have won more than 40 NCAA championships across a variety of sports. But they had never won a national title in men's tennis—until 2019, that is. After reaching the final against Wake Forest, Texas spotted the Demon Deacons the doubles point. But then the Longhorns swept through the singles matches to win 4–1.

VOLLEYBALL: Long Beach State

Four-time All-America selection **TJ DeFalco** was the star as Long Beach State outlasted Big West rival Hawaii in a taut 2019 championship match. Although the 49ers won the final by three sets to one, none of the four sets was decided by more than three points.

WATER POLO: USC

The Trojans entered the 2018 final with four consecutive title-game losses, including a couple in heartbreaking fashion. They weren't about to let it happen again. USC jumped out to a 5–0 lead in the opening moments and led

Minn. Duluth's Hunter Shepard

when it counted most, and they breezed past Massachusetts 3–0 in the 2019 final to win their second title in a row. Senior captain **Parker Mackay** had a goal and an assist in the final and was named the Frozen Four MVP. Goaltender **Hunter Shepard** posted the shutout while improving his career record to 8–0 in the NCAA Tournament.

Other National Champions

BASEBALL: **Vanderbilt**
CROSS COUNTRY: **Northern Arizona**
GOLF: **Stanford**
LACROSSE: **Virginia**
RIFLE (MEN AND WOMEN): **Texas Christian**
ROWING (MEN AND WUMEN): **Washington**
SKIING (MEN AND WOMEN): **Utah**
SWIMMING AND DIVING: **California**
TRACK AND FIELD (INDOOR): **Florida**
TRACK AND FIELD (OUTDOOR): **Texas Tech**
WRESTLING: **Penn State**

by as much as 12–4 before setting for a 14–12 win. Tournament MVP **Jacob Mercep** scored five goals to lead the Trojans to their tenth national title in water polo.

ICE HOCKEY: Minnesota Duluth

After winning the 2018 Frozen Four, the Bulldogs weren't always dominant in 2019. But they proved their mettle

Water polo players can never touch the bottom . . . but they can put the ball in the net!

Big Events 2019-20

September 2019

1 Rowing
Final day of World Championships, Ottensheim, Austria

5 Pro Football
The NFL's 100th regular season begins with Green Bay playing at Chicago

7–8 Tennis
US Open finals, New York, New York

11 Basketball
WNBA playoffs begin

22–29 Cycling
Road World Cycling Championships, Harrogate, United Kingdom

October 2019

1 Baseball
MLB postseason begins (Wild-Card playoff games, League Division Series, League Championship Series, World Series)

4 Ice Hockey
NHL regular season begins

4–13 Gymnastics
World Artistic Gymnastics Championships, Stuttgart, Germany

5 Ice Hockey
NWHL regular season begins

12 Swim/Bike/Run
Ironman Triathlon World Championship, Kailua-Kona, Hawaii

22 Basketball
NBA regular season begins

November 2019

3 Running
New York City Marathon

10 Soccer
MLS Cup, teams and site TBA

10–17 Tennis
ATP World Tour Finals, London, England

17 Stock Car Racing
Ford Ecoboost 400, final race of NASCAR Chase for the Sprint Cup, Homestead, Florida

24 Football
Grey Cup, CFL Championship Game, Calgary, Alberta, Canada

December 2019

1 Auto Racing
Abu Dhabi Grand Prix,
final race of Formula 1
season

5–14 Rodeo
National Finals Rodeo,
Las Vegas, Nevada

6 College Football
Pac-12 Championship Game,
Santa Clara, California

6, 8 College Soccer
Women's College Cup,
San Jose, California

7 College Football
ACC Championship Game,
Charlotte, North Carolina

Big 12 Championship Game,
Arlington, Texas

Big Ten Championship Game,
Indianapolis, Indiana

SEC Championship Game,
Atlanta, Georgia

12–15 Golf
Presidents Cup,
Melbourne, Australia

13, 15 College Soccer
Men's College Cup,
Cary, North Carolina

28 College Football
Cotton Bowl, Arlington,
Texas

College Football Playoff
Semifinal; Fiesta Bowl,
Glendale, Arizona

College Football Playoff
Semifinal; Peach Bowl, Atlanta,
Georgia

30 College Football
Orange Bowl, Miami, Florida

January 2020

1 College Football
Rose Bowl, Pasadena, California

Sugar Bowl, New Orleans,
Louisiana

4–5 Pro Football
NFL Wild Card Playoff
Weekend

11–12 Pro Football
NFL Divisional Playoff
Weekend

13 College Football
College Football Playoff
Championship Game,
New Orleans, Louisiana

19 Pro Football
NFL Conference Championship
Games

20–26 Figure Skating
US Figure Skating
Championships,
Greensboro, North Carolina

23–26 Action Sports
Winter X Games,
Aspen, Colorado

26 Hockey
NHL All-Star Game,
St. Louis, Missouri

26 Pro Football
NFL Pro Bowl, Location TBA

TBA Baseball
Caribbean Series,
Puerto Rico

February 2020

1–2 Tennis
Australian Open finals

2 Pro Football
Super Bowl LIV, South Florida

16 Basketball
NBA All-Star Game,
Chicago, Illinois

16 Stock Car Racing
(NASCAR) Daytona 500,
Daytona Beach, Florida

March 2020

13–15 Track and Field
IAAF World Indoor
Championships, Nanjing, China

16–22 Figure Skating
World Figure Skating
Championships, Montreal,
Quebec, Canada

26 Baseball
Major League Baseball,
Opening Day

April 2020

3, 5 College Basketball
NCAA Women's Final Four,
New Orleans, Louisiana

4, 6 College Basketball
NCAA Men's Final Four,
Atlanta, Georgia

9–12 Golf
The Masters,
Augusta, Georgia

TBA Ice Hockey
NHL playoffs begin

May 2020

2 Horse Racing
Kentucky Derby, Churchill
Downs, Louisville,
Kentucky

8–24 Ice Hockey
IIHF World Championships,
Switzerland

14–17 Golf
PGA Championship,
San Francisco, California

16 Horse Racing
Preakness Stakes,
Pimlico Race Course,
Baltimore, Maryland

24 IndyCar Racing
Indianapolis 500,
Indianapolis, Indiana

30 Soccer
UEFA Champions League Final,
Istanbul, Turkey

31– Tennis
June 1 French Open Finals,
Paris, France

June 2020

4–7 Golf
US Women's Open,
Houston, Texas

6 Horse Racing
Belmont Stakes,
Belmont Park,
Elmont, New York

12– Soccer
July 12 Copa América,
Argentina and Colombia

13 College Baseball
College World Series begins,
Omaha, Nebraska

18–21 Golf
US Open Championship,
Mamaroneck, New York

25–28 Golf
Women's PGA Championship,
Newtown Square,
Pennsylvania

27 Cycling
Tour de France begins,
Nice, France

TBA Basketball
NBA Finals, sites TBA

July 2020

11–12 Tennis
Wimbledon Championships
finals, London, England

14 Baseball
MLB All-Star Game,
Los Angeles, California

16–19 Action Sports
Summer X Games,
Minneapolis, Minnesota

16–19 Golf
British Open Championship,
Kent, England

24– Summer Olympic Games
Aug. 9 Tokyo, Japan

TBA Golf
Women's British Open
Championship, Troon, Scotland

August 2020

25– Summer Paralympics
Sept. 6 Tokyo, Japan

TBA Baseball
Little League World Series,
Williamsport, Pennsylvania

Note: Dates and sites subject to change. TBA: To be announced. Actual dates of event not available at press time.

Produced by Shoreline Publishing Group LLC

Santa Barbara, California

www.shorelinepublishing.com

President/Editorial Director: James Buckley, Jr.

Designed by Tom Carling, www.carlingdesign.com

The *Scholastic Year in Sports* text was written by

James Buckley, Jr.

Editorial assistance and text for Action Sports, Golf, Tennis, and Calendar: **Jim Gigliotti**.

NHL chapter: **Beth Adelman** and **Craig Zeichner**

Fact-checking: **Matt Marini**.

Thanks to team captain Amanda Shih, Jael Fogle, Emily Teresa, Marybeth Kavanagh, and the superstars at Scholastic for all their championship work! Photo research was done by the author.

Photography Credits

Photos ©: cover top left: Elaine Thompson/AP Images; cover center left: Bob DeChiara/USA TODAY Sports; cover center: Robert Deutsch/USA TODAY Sports; cover center right: Kevin C. Cox/Getty Images; cover bottom left: Elsa/Getty Images; cover bottom center: Ezra Shaw/Getty Images; cover bottom right: Jayne Kamin-Oncea/USA TODAY Sports; cover background: Aleksandr Artt/Shutterstock; cover top background: wanpatsorn/Shutterstock; back cover top center: Mark Rebilas/USA TODAY Sports; back cover top right: Erich Schlegel/USA TODAY Sports; back cover center left: Troy Taormina/USA TODAY Sports; back cover bottom left: Action Foto Sport/Getty Images; back cover bottom right: Darcy Finley/Getty Images; 4: Michael Chow/USA TODAY Sports; 5: Frank Augstein/AP Images; 6: Michael Woods/AP Images; 7: Vadim Ghirda/AP Images; 8: Eric Christian Smith/AP Images; 9: Kirby Lee/USA TODAY Sports; 10: Bob DeChiara/USA TODAY Sports; 11: Tim Spyers/Getty Images; 12: Lachlan Cunningham/AP Images; 13: Press Association/AP Images; 14-15: Michael Madrid/USA TODAY Sports; 16-17: Alessandra Tarantino/AP Images; 18-19: Matthew Emmons/USA TODAY Sports; 20: Quinn Harris/USA TODAY Sports; 21: Denny Medley/USA TODAY Sports; 22: Michael Ainsworth/AP Images; 23: David Butler II/USA TODAY Sports; 24: Gerald Herbert/AP Images; 25: Jason Getz/USA TODAY Sports; 26: Darron Cummings/AP Images; 27: NorthJersey.com/USA TODAY Sports; 28: Chuck Cook/USA TODAY Sports; 29: Chuck Cook/USA TODAY Sports; 30: Marcio Jose Sanchez/AP Images; 31: Jasen Vinlove/USA TODAY Sports; 32: Chuck Cook/USA TODAY Sports; 33: David Goldman/AP Images; 36-37: Kelley L Cox/USA TODAY Sports; 38: Thomas J. Russo/USA TODAY Sports; 39: Rich Graessle/AP Images; 40: Zach Bolinger/AP Images; 41: Chris Brown/AP Images; 42: Ron Chenoy/USA TODAY Sports; 43: Matthew Visinsky/AP Images; 44: Matt Kartozian/USA TODAY Sports; 45: David Morris/AP Images; 46: Steve Mitchell/USA TODAY Sports; 47: Matthew Emmons/USA TODAY Sports; 50-51: Paul Rutherford/USA TODAY Sports; 52: Benny Sieu/USA TODAY Sports; 53: Darren Yamashita/USA TODAY Sports; 54: Geoff Burke/USA TODAY Sports; 55: Evan Habeeb/USA TODAY Sports; 56: David Richard/USA TODAY Sports; 57: Jayne Kamin-Oncea/USA TODAY Sports; 58 top: Greg M. Cooper/USA TODAY Sports; 58 bottom: Robert Hanashiro/USA TODAY Sports; 59 top: Jayne Kamin-Oncea/USA TODAY Sports; 59 bottom: Gary A. Vasquez/USA TODAY Sports; 60: Charles LeClaire/USA TODAY Sports; 61: Kim Klement/USA TODAY Sports; 62 top: Richard Mackson/USA TODAY Sports; 62 bottom: Paul Sancya/AP Images; 63 top: Nate Billings/AP Images; 63 bottom: D. Ross Cameron/USA TODAY Sports; 66-67: Presse Sports/USA TODAY Sports; 68: Catherine Steenkeste/Getty Images; 69: Laurence Griffiths/Getty Images; 70: John Todd/Getty Images; 71: Zhizhao Wu/Getty Images; 72: Maja Hitij/Getty Images; 73: Alessandra Tarantino/AP Images; 74: Mark J. Rebilas/USA TODAY Sports; 75 top: Brett Davis/USA TODAY Sports; 75 bottom: Mark Graves/AP Images; 76 top: Denis Doyle/Getty Images; 76 bottom: VI Images/Getty Images; 77: VI Images/Getty Images; 80-81: Geoff Burke/USA TODAY Sports; 82: Matt Stamey/AP Images; 83: Jeffrey Brown/AP Images; 84: Rick Scuteri/AP Images; 85 top: Mark Humphrey/AP Images; 85 bottom: Marcio Jose Sanchez/AP Images; 86: Matt York/AP Images; 87 top: Jay Biggerstaff/USA TODAY Sports; 87 bottom: Brace Hemmelgarn/USA TODAY Sports; 88: Kim Klement/USA TODAY Sports; 89 top: Amanda Loman/AP Images; 89 bottom: Gregory Fisher/AP Images; 90: Chris O'Meara/AP Images; 91: Jasen Vinlove/USA TODAY Sports; 94-95: Frank Gunn/AP Images; 96: Brad Mills/USA TODAY Sports; 97: Quinn Harris/AP Images; 98: Ralph Freso/AP Images; 99 top: Jennifer Buchanan/USA TODAY Sports; 99 bottom: Brad Mills/USA TODAY Sports; 100: Jeff Hanisch/USA TODAY Sports; 101: Jaime Valdez/USA TODAY Sports; 102: Sue Ogrocki/AP Images; 103: Jason Getz/USA TODAY Sports; 104: Dan Hamilton/USA TODAY Sports; 105: Sergio Estrada/USA TODAY Sports; 106: John E. Sokolowski/USA TODAY Sports; 107: Carlos Osorio/AP Images; 110-111: Winslow Townson/USA TODAY Sports; 112: Kim Klement/USA TODAY Sports; 113: Jasen Vinlove/USA TODAY Sports; 114: Nick Wosika/AP Images; 115: Billy Hurst/USA TODAY Sports; 116: Aaron Doster/USA TODAY Sports; 117: Eric Canha/AP Images; 118: Anne-Marie Sorvin/USA TODAY Sports; 119: Nick Wass/AP Images; 122-123: Mike DiNovo/USA TODAY Sports; 124: Jerome Miron/USA TODAY Sports; 125: NKP, Russell LaBounty/AP Images; 126: Jim Dedmon/USA TODAY Sports; 127 left: Jasen Vinlove/USA TODAY Sports; 127 right: Terry Renna/AP Images; 128 top: Kelvin Kuo/USA TODAY Sports; 128 bottom: NKP, Russell LaBounty/AP Images; 129: John Raoux/AP Images; 132-133: Thomas J. Russo/USA TODAY Sports; 134 top left: Clive Mason/Getty Images; 134 top right: Dan Istitene/Getty Images; 134 bottom: Getty Images/Getty Images; 136: Stan Szeto/USA TODAY Sports; 137: Mark J. Rebilas/USA TODAY Sports; 138: MediaNews Group/Getty Images; 139 top: Charles Mitchell/Getty Images; 139 bottom: Thurman James/AP Images; 142-143: Sean M. Haffey/Getty Images; 144: Sean M. Haffey/Getty Images; 145: Sean M. Haffey/Getty Images; 147 top: Maddie Meyer/Getty Images; 147 bottom: Courtesy Bryce Carlson; 148: Michael Madrid/USA TODAY Sports; 149: Peter Casey/USA TODAY Sports; 150: David Cannon/Getty Images; 151: Chuck Burton/AP Images; 152: Kyodo/AP Images; 153 top: Mark J. Terrill/AP Images; 153 lemon: eugene4/Shutterstock; 153 bottom: Noah K. Murray/AP Images; 156: Presse Sports/USA TODAY Sports; 157: Tim Clayton/Corbis/Getty Images; 158: Susan Mullane/USA TODAY Sports; 159 bottom: Kyodo News/Getty Images; 159 top: Susan Mullane/USA TODAY Sports; 160: Professional Sport/Getty Images; 161: AFP/Getty Images; 162: Brian Rothmuller/AP Images; 163: Matthew Emmons/USA TODAY Sports; 164: Kevin Jairaj/USA TODAY Sports; 165: Ben Curtis/AP Images; 166: Kelvin Kuo/USA TODAY Sports; 167: Jake Roth/USA TODAY Sports; 168: Gregory Shamus/Getty Images; 169: Darryl Dyck/AP Images; 170: Dale Zanine/USA TODAY Sports; 171: Michael Gonzalez/Getty Images; 172-173: Ulrik Pedersen/Getty Images; 174: Jeff Curry/USA TODAY Sports; 175: Press Association/AP Images; 176 left: Mark Zerof/USA TODAY Sports; 176 right: John Minchillo/AP Images; 177: Larry MacDougal/AP Images; 178: Edith Geuppert//AP Images; 179 top: Kyodo News/AP Images; 179 bottom: Vadim Ghirda/AP Images; 180: Javier Soriano/Getty Images; 181 top: Michael Kappeler/Getty Images; 181 bottom: Atsushi Tomura/Getty Images; 182: Colin O'Brady; 183: Jono Searle/Getty Images; 184: Frank Jansky/AP Images; 185: Justin Tafoya/Getty Images; 186: Kelvin Kuo/USA TODAY Sports; 187 top: Gregory Fisher/AP Images; 187 bottom: Larry Placido/AP Images.